Revision  Guides

PEARSON
PUBLISHING

GCSE Mathematics

Higher Tier

Stafford Burndred

Consultant Editor: Brian Seager, Chairman of Examiners

GCSE Mathematics

Name...

Address ....

....

....

Date of exams: (1) ....

                                          (2) ....

                                          Aural ....

Coursework deadline dates: (1) ....

                                          (2) ....

Exam board ....

Syllabus number...

Candidate number ....

Centre number ....

Further copies of this publication, as well as the guides for Foundation and Intermediate tiers may be obtained from:

Pearson Publishing

Chesterton Mill, French's Road, Cambridge CB4 3NP

Tel 01223 350555   Fax 01223 356484

Email info@pearson.co.uk   Web site http://www.pearson.co.uk/education/

ISBN: 1 85749 377 X

Published by Pearson Publishing 1996

© Pearson Publishing

Contents

Contents

Contents

Introduction

The aim of this guide is to ensure you pass your exam and maybe even achieve a higher grade than you expect to. Ask your teacher to explain any points that you don't understand. You will have to work hard at your revision. Just reading this book will not be enough. You should also try to work through the tests at the back and any past papers that your teacher might set you to ensure that you get enough practice.

Remember it is your guide, so you may decide to personalise it, make notes in the margin, use the checklist in the contents to assess your progress, etc.

You may also find it useful to mark or highlight important sections, pages or questions you find difficult. You can then look at these sections again later.

The guide is divided into over 75 short topics to make it easy to revise. Try to set aside time every week to do some revision at home.

The guide is pocket-sized to make it easy to carry. Use it wherever you have time to spare, eg registration, break, etc.

Using the guide

It may help you to place a blank piece of paper over the answers. Then read the notes and try the questions.

Do your working out and answers on the blank piece of paper. Don't just read the answers. Compare your answers with the worked answer. If your answer is wrong read the page again and then mark or make a note of the question or page. You will need to try the question again at a later date.

If you need to look up a topic to revise, try using the contents pages, or even better, the index at the back of the book.

The diagnostic tests

Diagnostic tests and answers are provided at the back of the book. You should use these to identify your weaknesses.

The author has been teaching at this level for over 20 years and is an experienced examiner.

Examiner's tips

Success in exams depends in no small part on how you approach the actual papers on the day. The following suggestions are designed to improve your exam technique.

- Read carefully the instructions on the paper.

- If you only have to answer some of the questions, read the questions and choose which to do.

- If the instructions say "Answer all the questions", work steadily through the paper, leaving out any questions you cannot do. Return to these later.

- Read each question carefully to be sure what it is you are required to do.

- If your examination includes an oral test, be sure to follow the instructions and listen carefully. For some parts you must write down only the answer – no working!

- Set out all your work carefully and neatly and make your method clear. If the examiners can see what you have done, they will be able to give marks for the correct method even if you have the answer wrong.

- If you have to write an explanation as your answer, try to keep it short.

- There will be a list of formulae at the front of the question paper. Make sure you know what is on it, and what is not – you will have to remember those!

- Check your answers, especially numerical ones. Look to see if your answers are sensible.

- Make sure you know how to use your calculator. They don't all work in the same way. Use the instruction book for your calculator when you are learning but don't take it into the exam.

- When doing a calculation, keep all the figures shown on your calculator until the end. Only round off the final answer.

- Sometimes, in a later part of a question, you need to calculate using an earlier answer. Use all the figures in the calculator display. If you use a rounded answer it could cause an error.

- Make sure you take all the equipment you may need to the exam: pens, pencils, rubber, ruler, compasses, angle measurer and calculator – make sure that the battery is working.

- When you have completed the exam, check to see that you have not missed out any questions, especially on the back page.

Exam questions often use these words:

"Show your working"
You must show your working. If you give a correct answer without working you will receive no marks.

"Do not use a calculator"
You must show enough working to convince the examiner that you have not used a calculator. (But you should still check your answer with a calculator.)

"Check using an approximation" or *"Estimate"* or *"Give an approximate answer"*
You must show your method and working.

"Compare"
If you are asked to compare two sets of data you must refer to both sets of data and not just one set.

Avoiding panic

If you have done your revision you have no need to panic. If you find the examination difficult, so will everyone else. This means that the pass mark will be lower.

If you cannot do a question, move on and don't worry about it. Often the answer will come to you a few minutes later.

If panic occurs, try to find a question you can do. Success will help to calm your nerves.

The consultant editor is at the very hub of setting and marking GCSE Mathematics, being Chairman of Examiners after many years as a Chief Examiner.

Number skills

We use numbers every day of our lives. You need to be confident in the basic number skills.

Rational and irrational numbers

You are expected to know the difference between a rational and an irrational number.

A **rational** number is any number that can be written as a fraction.

Rational numbers include 5, -7, $\frac{3}{7}$, $5 \cdot 628$, $\sqrt{81}$, $\sqrt[3]{125}$, $7 \cdot \dot{3}$, $5 \cdot 2\dot{1}\dot{7}$

$$\boxed{\sqrt{81} = 9} \qquad \boxed{\sqrt[3]{125} = 5}$$

An **irrational** number is any number that cannot be written as a fraction.

Irrational numbers include:

Most square roots, eg $\sqrt{7}, \sqrt{8}$, (**not** $\sqrt{9}$ because 9 is a square number).

Most cube roots, eg $\sqrt[3]{18}$, $\sqrt[3]{20}$ (**not** $\sqrt[3]{64}$ because 64 is a cube number).

Almost anything involving π, eg $\frac{\pi}{2}$, 7π, but not $\frac{6\pi}{7\pi}$ because it cancels to give $\frac{6}{7}$

Note: $(2 + \sqrt{3})^2 = (2 + \sqrt{3})(2 + \sqrt{3})$	**Note:** Expansion of
$= 4 + 2\sqrt{3} + 2\sqrt{3} + 3 \leftarrow \sqrt{3} \times \sqrt{3} = 3$	brackets is explained
$= 7 + 4\sqrt{3}$	on page 16.

Recurring decimals are rational: Write the following recurring numbers as fractions:

$0 \cdot \dot{7} \quad = \quad 0 \cdot 777777 \quad = \quad \frac{7}{9} \quad$ 1 recurring number therefore 9 | **Note:** $0 \cdot 0\dot{7} = \frac{7}{90}$

$0 \cdot \dot{6}\dot{7} \quad = \quad 0 \cdot 676767 \quad = \quad \frac{67}{99} \quad$ 2 recurring numbers therefore 99

$0 \cdot \dot{4}2\dot{7} \quad = \quad 0 \cdot 427427 \quad = \quad \frac{427}{999} \quad$ 3 recurring numbers therefore 999

Questions

1. In each question state whether the number is rational or irrational. If the number is rational write the number in the form $\frac{a}{b}$.

    a $\sqrt{7}$ b $\dfrac{\sqrt{7}}{4\sqrt{7}}$ c $\sqrt{7} \times \sqrt{7}$

    d $0 \cdot \dot{4}$ e $0 \cdot 287$ f $0 \cdot 67$

    g 5π h $\sqrt{7} + \sqrt{7}$

2. $\sqrt{5} \times \sqrt{a}$ is rational. Find a possible value of a.

Answers

1. a   Irrational   b $\frac{1}{4}$ c   7   d $\frac{4}{9}$

    e $\frac{287}{999}$ f $\frac{67}{100}$ g   Irrational   h   Irrational

2. a = 5 or a = N x 5 where N is a square number   eg 16 x 5 = 80 (because $\sqrt{5} \times \sqrt{80} = 20$)

    (Other answers a = 20, 45, 80, 125...)

Calculator skills

Your calculator can be your best friend or your worst enemy. Spend some time learning to use it. You must buy a calculator with a fraction key $\boxed{a^b_c}$. You will be shown how to use a calculator but if the keys shown do not work ask your teacher for help.

Using a calculator: Brackets, memory and fractions

Most calculators automatically use algebraic logic and can work out the answers. Your task is to use the correct keys. You need to know how to use brackets – 'Method A' – and how to use the memory – 'Method B'.

Use of brackets

3 (6 + 8)   this means   3 x (6 + 8)

Calculator keys: $\boxed{3}$ $\boxed{x}$ $\boxed{(}$ $\boxed{6}$ $\boxed{+}$ $\boxed{8}$ $\boxed{)}$ $\boxed{=}$ Answer 42

(8 – 5) 3   this means   (8 – 5) x 3

Calculator keys: $\boxed{(}$ $\boxed{8}$ $\boxed{-}$ $\boxed{5}$ $\boxed{)}$ $\boxed{x}$ $\boxed{3}$ $\boxed{=}$ Answer 9

Questions involving division

Method A: Using brackets

$\dfrac{3\cdot86 - 4\cdot23}{7\cdot25 \times 3\cdot68}$ Place brackets at the start and end of the top line $\dfrac{(3\cdot86 - 4\cdot23)}{(7\cdot25 \times 3\cdot68)}$
Place brackets at the start and end of the bottom line

Calculator keys:

Answer – 0·013868065

Method B: Using the memory

First work out the answer to the bottom line (remember to press =).
Place this number in memory. Work out the answer to the top line. Divide by memory recall. Calculator keys: (look at your calculator instruction booklet if you do not know how to use the memory)   your memory key could say $\boxed{M^{IN}}$

Answer –0·013868065

Fractions $\boxed{a^b_c}$ key

$3\dfrac{4}{5} \times 2\dfrac{1}{4}$ Calculator keys:

$\boxed{3}$ $\boxed{a^b_c}$ $\boxed{4}$ $\boxed{a^b_c}$ $\boxed{5}$ $\boxed{x}$ $\boxed{2}$ $\boxed{a^b_c}$ $\boxed{1}$ $\boxed{a^b_c}$ $\boxed{4}$ $\boxed{=}$ Answer = $8\dfrac{11}{20}$

Using a calculator: Powers, roots and memory

Learn to use your calculator to do all of these calculations.

Use of power and root keys

Square key $\boxed{\mathbf{x^2}}$ This is used to square a number, eg $8^2 = 64$

Power key $\boxed{\mathbf{x^y}}$ or $\boxed{\mathbf{y^x}}$ This is used to calculate powers, eg 2^{-3}

Calculator keys: $\boxed{2}\ \boxed{x^y}\ \boxed{3}\ \boxed{+/-}\ \boxed{=}$ Answer 0·125

Square root $\boxed{\sqrt{\ }}$ This is used to calculate the square root of a number, eg $\sqrt{36} = 6$

Cube root $\boxed{\sqrt[3]{\ }}$ This is used to calculate the cube root of a number, eg $\sqrt[3]{125} = 5$

Root key $\boxed{\sqrt[x]{\ }}$ or $\boxed{x^{\frac{1}{y}}}$ This is used to calculate the root of a number, eg $\sqrt[5]{32} = 2$

Calculator keys: $\boxed{3}\ \boxed{2}\ \boxed{x^{\frac{1}{y}}}\ \boxed{5}\ \boxed{=}$ Answer 2

Use of memory

Most calculators use: $\boxed{M}$ to put into memory. $\boxed{MR}$ is used to recall what is in memory.

If you need to use a number more than once it may help reduce the calculation by saving the number in memory. But remember: When you put a number into memory, you will lose the previous number in memory.

Questions

1   Calculate $8^2 + 5^2$ 2   What is the value of 4^5?

3   A square has an area of 81 cm^2. What is the length of each side?

4   A cube has a volume of 64 cm^3. What is the length of each side?

5   $y = 3x^3 + 4x^2 + 2x$. Calculate the value of y when x = 2·974

6   Calculate $\sqrt[4]{16}$ 7   Calculate 4^{-2}

Answers

1   Calculator keys $\boxed{8}\ \boxed{x^2}\ \boxed{+}\ \boxed{5}\ \boxed{x^2}\ \boxed{=}$ Answer 89

2   Calculator keys $\boxed{4}\ \boxed{x^y}\ \boxed{5}\ \boxed{=}$ Answer 1024

3   Calculator keys $\boxed{8}\ \boxed{1}\ \boxed{\sqrt{\ }}$ Answer 9 cm

4   Calculator keys $\boxed{6}\ \boxed{4}\ \boxed{\sqrt[3]{\ }}$ Answer 4 cm

5   First put 2.974 into memory.   Calculator keys $\boxed{2}\ \boxed{\cdot}\ \boxed{9}\ \boxed{7}\ \boxed{4}\ \boxed{M}$

    Calculator keys $\boxed{3}\ \boxed{\times}\ \boxed{MR}\ \boxed{x^y}\ \boxed{3}\ \boxed{+}\ \boxed{4}\ \boxed{\times}\ \boxed{MR}\ \boxed{x^2}\ \boxed{+}\ \boxed{2}\ \boxed{\times}\ \boxed{MR}\ \boxed{=}$

         Answer 120.24

6   Calculator keys $\boxed{1}\ \boxed{6}\ \boxed{x^{\frac{1}{y}}}\ \boxed{4}\ \boxed{=}$ Answer 2

7   Calculator keys $\boxed{4}\ \boxed{x^y}\ \boxed{2}\ \boxed{+/-}\ \boxed{=}$ Answer 0·0625

Standard form

Standard form is used to write very large and very small numbers.

$5\cdot36 \times 10^{4}$

Means move the decimal point
4 places to the right

$5\,3\,6\,0\,0' = 53\;600$

> In standard form a number is written in the form:
> $a \times 10^{n}$
> Where a is a number between 1 and 10 and n is an appropriate power of 10

$8\cdot31 \times 10^{-3}$

Means move the decimal point
3 places to the left

$0\,0\,0\,8\,3\,1 = 0\cdot00831$

Using a calculator with numbers in standard form

> Use the $\boxed{\text{EXP}}$ or $\boxed{\text{EE}}$ key
>
> Example $3\cdot82 \times 10^{4} \times 4\cdot26 \times 10^{6}$
>
> Calculator keys:
>
> $\boxed{3}\;\boxed{.}\;\boxed{8}\;\boxed{2}\;\boxed{\text{EXP}}\;\boxed{4}\;\boxed{\text{x}}$
> $\boxed{4}\;\boxed{.}\;\boxed{2}\;\boxed{6}\;\boxed{\text{EXP}}\;\boxed{6}\;\boxed{=}$
>
> The calculator display shows
> $1\cdot62732\,^{11}$
> This means $1\cdot62732 \times 10^{11}$

Questions

1   Write 8.4×10^{3} as an ordinary number.

2   Write $3\cdot24 \times 10^{-2}$ as an ordinary number.

3   Write 3820 in standard form.

4   Write 0·00236 in standard form.

5   $7\cdot3 \times 10^{8} \div 6\cdot4 \times 10^{-7}$

Answers

1   $8\,4\,0\,0' = 8400$ 2 $0\,0\,3\,2\,4 = 0\cdot0324$

3   Note: In standard form the decimal point is always after the first whole number.

   $3\,8\,2\,0$ The decimal point has moved 3 places to the left.
   We write the number in standard form as $3\cdot82 \times 10^{3}$

4   $0\cdot0\,0\,2\,3\,6$ The decimal point has moved 3 places to the right.
   We write the number in standard form as $2\cdot36 \times 10^{-3}$

5      Answer $1\cdot140625 \times 10^{15}$

   Common error:
   Do not put $\boxed{\text{x}}\;\boxed{1}\;\boxed{0}$ into your calculator. $\boxed{\text{EXP}}$ does this.

   > Another common error is to write $1\cdot140625^{15}$.
   > This will lose marks. You must write $1\cdot140625 \times 10^{15}$

Fractions, decimals and percentages

This section is a lot easier than you think. A variety of methods, including calculator methods are shown.

Percentages and fractions

You have to be able to work out percentages. Shops often have sales with 20% off. If you cannot do percentages you cannot work out the sale price.

> To find 6%, multiply by 0·06
> To calculate a 6% increase, multiply by 1·06 (ie 1 + 0·06)
> To calculate a 12% decrease, multiply by 0·88 (ie 1 − 0·12)
> To calculate $^2/_3$, multiply by $^2/_3$
> To calculate a $^2/_3$ increase, multiply by $1^2/_3$ (ie 1 + $^2/_3$)
> To calculate a $^2/_3$ decrease, multiply by $^1/_3$ (ie 1 − $^2/_3$)

Examples

1   A man earns £12 000 per annum. He receives a 4% increase each year. How much does he earn after five years?

Method: 12 000 x 1·04 x 1·04 x 1·04 x 1·04 x 1·04 = £14 599·83
A shortcut is: 12 000 x $1·04^5$ = £14 599·83

2   A television costs £200 + 17·5% VAT. What is the total cost?
200 x 1·175 = £235

This is a common examination question:

A television costs £235 including 17·5% VAT. Calculate the cost before VAT was added.

£235 is 117·5%. We need to find 100%. It is example 2 reversed. 235 ÷ 1·175 = £200

Questions

1   A car is bought for £15 000. It depreciates by 9% each year. How much is it worth after three years? (Give your answer to the nearest £.)

2   Decrease 48 by $^1/_3$ 3   Find 8% of 20

Answers

1   15 000   x   0·91   x   0·91   x   0·91   =   £11 304

            ↑   ↑   ↑
     to find the   to find the   to find the
     value after   value after   value after
     one year   two years   three years

The calculation can be shortened   15 000 x $(0·91)^3$
Calculator keys: [1] [5] [0] [0] [0] [x] [0] [·] [9] [1] [x'] [3] [=]

2   Decrease by $^1/_3$ means multiply by (1 − $^1/_3$) = $^2/_3$ 48 x $^2/_3$ = 32

3   Find 8% means multiply by 0·08 ⟶ 0·08 x 20 = 1·6

5

Calculating growth and decay rates

Some amounts increase by a fixed amount over a fixed period of time. This fixed amount is the growth rate, eg a population may increase by 5% each year. Some amounts decrease by a fixed amount each year. This is called the decay rate, eg radioactive material may decay by 3% each year.

Important: If you are going forward in time **multiply**, it you are going back in time **divide**

Example

A man's salary increased by 6% per year. In 1985 he earned £12 000. In which year did his salary first exceed £18 000?

Method

A 6% increase means multiply by 1·06 (ie 1 + 0·06)

12 000   x   1.06   x   1.06   x   etc

             ↑   ↑

      salary in 1986   salary in 1987

this will work but it will take a long time. A quicker way is trial and improvement.

$12\ 000 \times 1.06^n$ ← number of years

try n = 10	£12 000 x 1.06^{10} = £21 490 too high
try n = 8	£12 000 x 1.06^{8} = £19 126 too high
try n = 6	£12 000 x 1.06^{6} = £17 022 too low
try n = 7	£12 000 x 1.06^{7} = £18 044 first year salary exceeded £18000

Answer = 1992

Question

1   An island had 15 000 seals in 1980. The seal population is decreasing by 2% each year:

   a   What was the population in 1986?

   b   When will the population fall below 10 000?

   c   What was the population in 1970?

Answers

1   a   15 000 x 0.98^6 = 13 288 (**Note:** Going **forward** in time **multiply**)

   b   Use trial and improvement (see example) 15000 x 0.98^{21} = 9814   ← in 21 years →   Answer = Year 2001

   c   15 000 ÷ 0.98^{10} = 18 358 (**Note:** Going **back** in time **divide**)

Number patterns

In this section you will find some patterns which may help you with your coursework projects. Learn the number patterns, eg square numbers.

Patterns you must recognise

These number patterns often appear in coursework and on examination papers. Life is much easier if you recognise them immediately. Learn these number patterns. They will help you to stay one step ahead of the examiner.

Square numbers

(eg 6 x 6 = 36, therefore 36 is a square number) **Note:** 6 is the square root of 36

etc

| 1, | 4, | 9, | 16, | 25, | 36, | 49, | 64, | 81, | 100 |

Cube numbers

(eg 5 x 5 x 5 = 125, therefore 125 is a cube number) **Note:** 5 is the cube root of 125

etc

| 1, | 8, | 27, | 64, | 125, | 216, | 343, | 512, | 729, | 1000 |

Triangle numbers

etc

| 1, | 3, | 6, | 10, | 15, | 21, | 28, | 36, | 45, | 55 |
| (1) | (1+2) | (1+2+3) | (1+2+3+4) | etc | | | | | |

Fibonacci sequence

(Add the two previous terms in the sequence).

| 1, | 1, | 2, | 3, | 5, | 8, | 13, | 21, | 34, | 55 |
| | | (1+1=2) | (1+2=3) | (2+3=5) | (3+5=8) | (5+8=13) | etc | | |

Information you should know

Multiples: The multiples of 3 are 3, 6, 9, 12, 15...
Any number in the 3 times table is a multiple of 3, eg 36, 42, 300.

Factors: The factors of 12 are 1, 2, 3, 4, 6, 12
Any number which divides exactly into 12 is a factor of 12.

Prime numbers: Prime numbers have **exactly two** factors.
The prime numbers are 2, 3, 5, 7, 11, 13, 17, 19...

Note: 1 is not a prime number because it has only one factor.

Product of primes, highest common factor, lowest common multiple and reciprocals

There are many ways of calculating the highest common factor (HCF) and lowest common multiple (LCM). If you have your own method and it works stick with it. If not use the methods below:

Reciprocals

A number multiplied by its reciprocal equals 1.

The reciprocal of $^2/_3$ is $^3/_2$ (ie $^2/_3$ x $^3/_2$ = 1)

To find a reciprocal turn the number upside down, eg reciprocal of $^3/_4$ is $^4/_3$

Reciprocal of –4 is $–^1/_4$ (**Note:** –4 means $–^4/_1$)

Questions

1 Write 1176 as a product of primes.

2 Find the HCF and LCM of 1176 and 420.

3 What is the reciprocal of 5?

Answers

1 (Remember prime numbers are 2, 3, 5, 7, 11, 13...)

Keep dividing 1176 by the prime numbers, starting with 2, then 3, then 5, etc.

```
2 | 1176
2 |  588
2 |  294
3 |  147  ◄──── (2 will not go into 147, so try 3)
7 |   49  ◄──── (3 will not go into 49, so try 5)
                (5 will not go into 49, so try 7)
7 |    7
       1  ◄──── Note: Keep dividing by prime numbers until you get to 1
```

The prime factors of 1176 are 2 x 2 x 2 x 3 x 7 x 7 = 2^3 x 3 x 7^2 = $2^3.3.7^2$

Note: The use of the dot is a quicker method of indicating 'multiply'

2 Write 1176 as a product of primes (see above) 2 x 2 x 2 x 3 x 7 x 7

then write 420 as a product of primes 2 x 2 x 3 x 5 x 7

HCF (factors in both)	2	x	2			x	3		x	7			= **84**
1176 =	2	x	2	x	2	x	3			x	7	x	7
420 =	2	x	2			x	3	x	5	x	7		
LCM (maximum number of factors)	2	x	2	x	2	x	3	x	5	x	7	x	7	= **5880**

3 $^1/_5$

A variety of techniques are shown.

Trial and improvement

This used to be called trial and error. But mathematicians do not like errors so they changed the name to improvement. Make sure you remember the four columns.

WARNING: This topic can be a time-waster in the examination. If you are short of time this is a question to leave and go back to at the end.

Trial and improvement

You should draw four columns as shown below.

In the first column write down your guess. In the second column work out the answer using your guess.

Advice: Always write the question with the letters on one side, numbers on the other side, eg if the question states solve $x^3 = 2x^2 + 25$ by trial and improvement rewrite the question as $x^3 - 2x^2 = 25$ then proceed as shown in the answer below.

If your answer is too big write your **guess** in the 'too big' column.
If your answer is too small write your **guess** in the 'too small' column.

Guess x	Answer	Too big	Too small

Question

$x^3 + 2x = 161$

Find the value of x correct to one decimal place using trial and improvement methods.

Answer

You must show your working. For example, start by guessing 5. You may have used different guesses in your calculations.

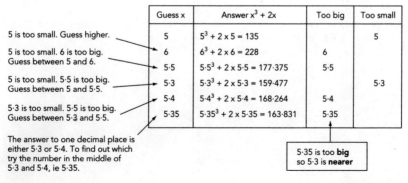

	Guess x	Answer $x^3 + 2x$	Too big	Too small
5 is too small. Guess higher.	5	$5^3 + 2 \times 5 = 135$		5
5 is too small. 6 is too big. Guess between 5 and 6.	6	$6^3 + 2 \times 6 = 228$	6	
	5·5	$5·5^3 + 2 \times 5·5 = 177·375$	5·5	
5 is too small. 5·5 is too big. Guess between 5 and 5·5.	5·3	$5·3^3 + 2 \times 5·3 = 159·477$		5·3
	5·4	$5·4^3 + 2 \times 5·4 = 168·264$	5·4	
5·3 is too small. 5·5 is too big. Guess between 5·3 and 5·5.	5·35	$5·35^3 + 2 \times 5·35 = 163·831$	5·35	

The answer to one decimal place is either 5·3 or 5·4. To find out which try the number in the middle of 5·3 and 5·4, ie 5·35.

5·35 is too **big** so 5·3 is **nearer**

Answer = 5·3

Equations

Look at this: $\sqrt{16} = 4$ and $4^2 = 16$

therefore $16 = 4^2$ $4 = \sqrt{16}$

This is how it works in equations: $\sqrt{A} = 6$ and $C^2 = 80$

therefore $A = 6^2$ $C = \sqrt{80}$

$A = 36$ $C = 8\cdot94$ (approx)

(or $-8\cdot94$)

Note: All numbers have two square roots. One is positive and one is negative, ie $\sqrt{25}$ is $+5$ **or** -5

The following questions show several useful techniques. For each question find the value of y correct to three significant figures where appropriate.

Questions

1 $y^2 = 10$

2 $\sqrt{y} = 30$

3 $\sqrt{y} - 3 = 8$

4 $5(y + 3) = 3(4y - 2)$

5 $6y - 4(2y - 3) = 10$

6 $^5/_y + 2 = 6$

Answers

1 $y^2 = 10$
$y = \sqrt{10}$
$y = 3\cdot16$ (or $-3\cdot16$)

2 $\sqrt{y} = 30$
$y = 30^2$
$y = 900$

3 $\sqrt{y} - 3 = 8$
$\sqrt{y} = 8 + 3$
$\sqrt{y} = 11$
$y = 11^2$
$y = 121$

4 $5(y + 3) = 3(4y - 2)$
$5y + 15 = 12y - 6$
$5y - 12y = -6 - 15$
$-7y = -21$
$y = {}^{-21}/_{-7}$
$y = 3$

5 $6y - 4(2y - 3) = 10$
$6y - 8y + 12 = 10$
$6y - 8y = 10 - 12$
$-2y = -2$
$y = {}^{-2}/_{-2}$
$y = 1$

6 $^5/_y + 2 = 6$
$^5/_y = 6 - 2$
$^5/_y = 4$
$5 = 4y$
$^5/_4 = y$
$1\cdot25 = y$

Rewriting formulae

I have shown questions you may be given and the techniques for solving them.

> **Look at this:** $\sqrt{16} = 4$ and $4^2 = 16$
>
> therefore $16 = 4^2$ $4 = \sqrt{16}$
>
> **This is how it works in formulae:** $\sqrt{C} = D$ and $E^2 = H$
>
> therefore $C = D^2$ $E = \sqrt{H}$

The following questions show several useful techniques.
In each question make A the subject.

Questions

1 $\sqrt{A} = B$ 2 $A^2 = B$ 3 $3C\sqrt{A} = B$

4 $C = B + A$ 5 $C = B - A$ 6 $C = \dfrac{A}{B}$

7 $C = \dfrac{B}{A}$ 8 $AB + C = D$ 9 $3B = \dfrac{Y}{2A} - 7$

10 $3B = \dfrac{Y - 7}{2A}$ 11 $V = \dfrac{1}{3} \pi r^2 h$ Make r the subject

Answers

1 $\sqrt{A} = B$
  $A = B^2$

2 $A^2 = B$
  $A = \sqrt{B}$

3 $3C\sqrt{A} = B$
  $\sqrt{A} = \dfrac{B}{3C}$
  $A = \left(\dfrac{B}{3C}\right)^2$

4 $C = B + A$
  $B + A = C$
  $A = C - B$

5 $C = B - A$
  $C + A = B$
  $A = B - C$

6 $C = \dfrac{A}{B}$
  $\dfrac{A}{B} = C$
  $A = BC$

7 $C = \dfrac{B}{A}$
  $AC = B$
  $A = \dfrac{B}{C}$

8 $AB + C = D$
  $AB = D - C$
  $A = \dfrac{D - C}{B}$

9 $3B = \dfrac{Y}{2A} - 7$
  $3B + 7 = \dfrac{Y}{2A}$
  $A(3B + 7) = \dfrac{Y}{2}$
  $A = \dfrac{Y}{2(3B + 7)}$

10 $3B = \dfrac{Y - 7}{2A}$
  $3AB = \dfrac{Y - 7}{2}$
  $A = \dfrac{Y - 7}{2(3B)}$
  $A = \dfrac{Y - 7}{6B}$

11 $V = \dfrac{1}{3} \pi r^2 h$
  $3V = \pi r^2 h$
  $\left(\dfrac{3V}{\pi h}\right) = r^2$
  $r = \sqrt{\left(\dfrac{3V}{\pi h}\right)}$

Iteration

Iteration is a process of repeating a sequence of instructions to produce a better and better approximation to the correct answer. A converging sequence gets closer and closer to a solution. A diverging sequence does not.

Solving quadratic equations by iterative methods

Example 1

Find the iterative formulae to solve $x^2 + 2x - 8 = 0$

> **Note:** Factorisation is explained on page 17.

Method: Put x terms to the left of equals; numbers to the right of equals.

$$\text{Factorise} \quad x(x + 2) = 8$$

$$\textbf{Either} \quad x = \frac{8}{x + 2} \quad \textbf{or} \quad x + 2 = \frac{8}{x}$$

$$x = \frac{8}{x} - 2$$

These give the iterative formulae $x_{n+1} = \frac{8}{x_n + 2}$ or $x_{n+1} = \frac{8}{x_n} - 2$

Example 2

Use the iterative formula $x_{n+1} = \frac{8}{x_n + 2}$ to solve $x^2 + 2x - 8 = 0$

$$\text{Start with} \quad x_1 = 1 \qquad x_{n+1} = \frac{8}{1 + 2} \quad = 2 \cdot 667$$

$$x_2 = 2 \cdot 667 \qquad x_{n+1} = \frac{8}{2 \cdot 667 + 2} \quad = 1 \cdot 714$$

$$x_3 = 1 \cdot 714 \qquad \text{and continue...} \quad \text{Eventually we find the solution is } x = 2$$

Questions

1. Produce two iterative formulae for $x^2 + 4x - 12 = 0$

2. Use the formula $x_{n+1} = \frac{8}{x_n} - 2$ with a starting value of $x_1 = -3$
   to find a solution to $x^2 + 2x - 8 = 0$ correct to 2 decimal places.

Answers

1. $x^2 + 4x = 12$
   $x(x + 4) = 12$
   $$x_{n+1} = \frac{12}{x_n + 4} \quad \text{or} \quad x + 4 = \frac{12}{x}$$
   $$x_{n+1} = \frac{12}{x_n} - 4$$

2. You should obtain these values:
   $x_2 = -4 \cdot 666...$
   $x_3 = -3 \cdot 714...$
   $x_4 = -4 \cdot 153...$
   Eventually we find the answer.
   Answer $x = -4 \cdot 00$

Variation

This page shows a useful mathematical technique.

Direct and inverse variation

These statements all mean the same:

a ∝ b
a is proportional to b
a varies as b
a varies directly as b

$a \propto \frac{1}{b}$ means a is **inversely** proportional to b

Direct variation

a ∝ b	this means	$a = kb$
a ∝ b²	this means	$a = kb^2$
a ∝ b³	this means	$a = kb^3$

These are the "k" equations for direct variation

Inverse variation

$a \propto \frac{1}{b}$	this means	$a = \frac{k}{b}$
$a \propto \frac{1}{b^2}$	this means	$a = \frac{k}{b^2}$
$a \propto \frac{1}{b^3}$	this means	$a = \frac{k}{b^3}$

These are the "k" equations for inverse variation

Example

y is proportional to x^2. y = 75 when x = 5. Find the value of:

    a   y when x = 7   b   x when y = 192

Method

First write out the equation and find the value of k

$$y = kx^2$$
$$75 = k \times 5^2$$
$$\frac{75}{25} = k$$
$$k = 3$$

a Write out the k equation

$$y = kx^2$$
$$y = 3 \times 7^2$$
$$y = 147$$

b Write out the k equation

$$y = kx^2$$
$$192 = 3 x^2$$
$$\frac{192}{3} = x^2$$
$$64 = x^2$$
$$\sqrt{64} = x$$
$$x = 8$$

Question

y is inversely proportional to x^2. y = 8 when x = 5. Find the value of y when x = 2.

Answer

First write out the equation and find the value of k

$$y = \frac{k}{x^2}$$
$$8 = \frac{k}{5^2}$$
$$8 \times 25 = k$$
$$k = 200$$

Write out the k equation

$$y = \frac{k}{x^2}$$
$$y = \frac{200}{2^2}$$
$$y = 50$$

Algebraic skills

People tend not to like algebra. It is difficult to understand and even more difficult to explain. I have tried to make it as simple as I can.

Using algebraic formulae

Example

Find D given   a = 3·2   b = 5·4   c = –2·1

$$D = \sqrt{\left(\frac{3a - 2c}{a + c}\right)}$$

Method   First write the question replacing the letters with numbers.

$$D = \sqrt{\left(\frac{3 \times 3·2 - 2 \times -2·1}{3·2 + -2·1}\right)}$$

Look at *Using a calculator* (page 2).

Work out everything in the brackets.
Remember to put brackets at the start and end of each line.

$$\frac{(3 \times 3·2 - 2 \times -2·1)}{(3·2 + -2·1)}$$

Calculator keys:

(3 × 3 · 2 − 2 × 2 · 1 +/−) ÷
(3 · 2 + 2 · 1 +/−)

Now press = and finally √ Answer 3·54...

Note: If you are finding a square root the last two keys will be = √

Question

Calculate the value of r given v = 90, h = 6 and $v = \frac{1}{3} \pi r^2 h$

Answer

First rewrite the formula making r the subject (see Question 11 on page 11)

$$r = \sqrt{\left(\frac{3v}{\pi h}\right)} \qquad r = \sqrt{\left(\frac{3 \times 90}{\pi \times 6}\right)}$$

Calculator keys:

(3 × 9 0) ÷ (π × 6) = √

Answer 3·78 (approx)

Rules for indices (powers)

$a^3 \times a^4 = (a \times a \times a) \times (a \times a \times a \times a) = a^7$. Here are some rules to help you.

Indices (powers)

$a^3 \times a^4 = a^7$ If it is multiplication **add** the powers: $3 + 4 = 7$

$a^8 \div a^6 = a^2$ If it is division **subtract** the powers: $8 - 6 = 2$

$(a^5)^3 = a^{15}$ **Multiply** the powers: $5 \times 3 = 15$

$5a^4 \times 3a^6 = 15a^{10}$ **Multiply** the whole numbers and **add** the powers

$8a^3 \div 2a^8 = 4a^{-5}$ **Divide** the whole numbers and **subtract** the powers

| **Note:** | $y^{-3} = \dfrac{1}{y^3}$ | $5a^2$ means $5 \times a \times a$
 $(5a)^2$ means $5a \times 5a = 25a^2$ | $\sqrt[5]{y} = y^{1/5}$ |

Questions

Simplify:

1   $y^3 \times y^5$ 2 $y^4 \div y^{-5}$ 3 $y^{1/3} \times y^{2/5}$

4   $y^{-1/2} \times y^{-2/5}$ 5 $y^{1/3} \div y^{1/2}$ 6 $y^{-2/5} \div y^{-3/8}$

Evaluate:

7   8^{-2} 8 $\sqrt[7]{128}$

9   5^0 10 6^1

Answers

1   $y^{3+5} = y^8$ 2 $y^{4--5} = y^9$ 3 $y^{1/3+2/5} = y^{11/15}$

4   $y^{(-1/2+-2/5)} = y^{-9/10}$ 5 $y^{(1/3-1/2)} = y^{-1/6}$ 6 $y^{(-2/5-3/8)} = y^{-1/40}$

7   Calculator keys:

     $\boxed{8}\ \boxed{x^y}\ \boxed{2}\ \boxed{+/-}\ \boxed{=}$

An alternative solution is:

$8^{-2} = \dfrac{1}{8^2} = \dfrac{1}{64}$

Answer = 0·015625

8   Calculator keys:

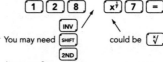

You may need $\boxed{\text{SHIFT}}$ could be $\boxed{\sqrt[x]{\ }}$

Answer = 2

9   At GCSE you can assume any number to the power of 0 is 1

$5^0 = 1$ $7^0 = 1$

$-3^0 = 1$ $0·27^0 = 1$

10   Any number to the power of 1 is itself

$6^1 = 6$ $8^1 = 8$

$-3^1 = -3$ $0·56^1 = 0·56$

Expansion of brackets

Expansion of brackets

Example: $5y^3(3y^4 + 2ay)$ this means $5y^3 \times 3y^4 + 5y^3 \times 2ay = 15y^7 + 10ay^4$

Questions

1 $3a^5 \times 2a^4 =$ 2 $5a^6 \times 2a =$

3 $3a^2cy^3 \times 4ac^5y^{-5} =$ 4 $12a^3cd^8 \div 3ac^3d^2 =$

Expand the following:

5 $5(2a - 3)$ 6 $3a(5 - 6a)$

7 $4y^6(2y^3 + 4y^2)$ 8 $-3(a^3 + 2y^2)$

9 $4a^3b^2cd^2(3ab^4 - 6ac^3d)$ 10 $(3a + 2)(5a - 3)$

11 $(6a - 7)(4a - 3)$ 12 $(4y - 3)(7y + 6)$

13 $(6a - 4)^2$

Answers

1 $6a^9$

2 $10a^7$ **(Note: 2a means $2a^1$)**

3 $12a^3c^6y^{-2}$ $\left[\text{or } \dfrac{12a^3c^6}{y^2} \right]$

4 $4a^2c^{-2}d^6$ $\left[\text{or } \dfrac{4a^2d^6}{c^2} \right]$

5 $5(2a - 3)$
   $10a - 15$

6 $3a(5 - 6a)$
   $15a - 18a^2$

7 $4y^6(2y^3 + 4y^2)$
   $8y^9 + 16y^8$

8 $-3(a^3 + 2y^2)$
   $-3a^3 - 6y^2$

9 $4a^3b^2cd^2(3ab^4 - 6ac^3d)$
   $12a^4b^6cd^2 - 24a^4b^2c^4d^3$

10 $(3a + 2)(5a - 3)$
    $3a(5a - 3) + 2(5a - 3)$
    $15a^2 - 9a + 10a - 6$
    $15a^2 + a - 6$

11 $(6a - 7)(4a - 3)$
    $6a(4a - 3) - 7(4a - 3)$
    $24a^2 - 18a - 28a + 21$
    $24a^2 - 46a + 21$
    Note: $-7 \times -3 = 21$

12 $(4y - 3)(7y + 6)$
    $4y(7y + 6) - 3(7y + 6)$
    $28y^2 + 24y - 21y - 18$
    $28y^2 + 3y - 18$
    Note: $-3 \times 6 = -18$

13 $(6a - 4)^2$
    This means:
    $(6a - 4)(6a - 4)$
    $6a(6a - 4) - 4(6a - 4)$
    $36a^2 - 24a - 24a + 16$
    $36a^2 - 48a + 16$

Factorisation – 1

You must complete "Expansion of brackets" before factorisation. Factorisation is the reverse operation to expansion of brackets.

Example

Expand $4(2a + 1)$

           $8a + 4$

Factorise $8a + 4$

             $4(2a + 1)$

> Factorising means finding common factors
>
> $$6a + 15$$
>
> 3 is a factor of 6 and 15
>
> $$3(2a + 5)$$

Questions

Factorise:

1   $30c^2 - 12c$

2   $15c^2d + 20c^5d^4$

3   $6a^2bc^3 + 4a^4b^2d$

Answers

1   6 is the highest number that goes into 30 and 12 (ie the highest factor)

    c is the highest power of c that goes into c^2 and c

    $6c(5c - 2)$

2

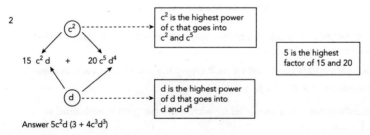

Answer $5c^2d(3 + 4c^3d^3)$

3   2 is the highest number that goes into 6 and 4

    a^2 is the highest power of a that goes into a^2 and a^4

    b is the highest power of b that goes into b and b^2

    $2a^2b(3c^3 + 2a^2bd)$

Factorisation – 2

This page shows the rules when two sets of brackets are required.

Rules for the factorisation of more difficult questions

Look at the last sign.

If the **last** sign is + (positive) then the signs in the brackets will both be the same as the **previous** sign.

If the **last** sign is – (negative) then the signs in the brackets will be **different,** ie one will be + and the other will be –. For example:

Previous sign   Last sign

1   Factorise $x^2 + 5x + 6$ ⟶ $(x + 3)(x + 2)$

2   Factorise $x^2 - 5x + 6$ ⟶ $(x - 3)(x - 2)$

3   Factorise $x^2 + 5x - 6$ ⟶ $(x + 6)(x - 1)$

4   Factorise $x^2 - 5x - 6$ ⟶ $(x - 6)(x + 1)$

Example

Factorise $a^2 - 7a + 10$. Last sign is +, therefore the signs in the brackets will both be the same as the previous sign, ie – (negative).

Multiply these to produce the first term, ie a^2

$$(\ - \ )(\ - \ )$$

Multiply these to produce the last term, ie 10

The first term: a^2 is produced by multiplying the first term in each bracket. The only possibility is a x a.

The last term: 10 is produced by multiplying the last term in each bracket. Possibilities are 1 x 10, 2 x 5, 5 x 2, 10 x 1.

The middle term: –7a is produced by adding the last term in each bracket,

ie $-1 + -10 = -11$
     $-2 + -5 = -7$ ⟶ this works
     $-5 + -2 = -7$ ⟶ this works
     $-10 + -1 = -11$

Solution: $(a - 2)(a - 5)$ **or** $(a - 5)(a - 2)$

Note: You can check the answer by expanding the brackets (see page 16, Question 10). Expanding $(a - 2)(a - 5)$ gives the expression in the question, ie $a^2 - 7a + 10$.

Factorisation – 3

$a^2 - b^2$ factorises as $(a + b)(a - b)$

Example

Factorise $x^2 - 36$

Answer $= (x + 6)(x - 6)$ **Note:** 6 is the square root of 36

Questions

1   Factorise $y^2 - 2y - 8$

2   Solve $y^2 - 2y - 8 = 0$ by factorisation

Answers

Last sign is negative.

↓

1   $y^2 - 2y - 8$

Therefore the signs in the brackets are different.

$y \times y = y^2$

$(y + \quad)(y - \quad)$ Middle term (ie $-2y$)

+ 1	– 8	→	+ 1 – 8 = –7
+ 2	– 4	→	+ 2 – 4 = –2 Correct solution
+ 4	– 2	→	+ 4 – 2 = 2
+ 8	– 1	→	+ 8 – 1 = 7

Answer $(y + 2)(y - 4)$

2   First factorise (see above)

$(y + 2)(y - 4) = 0$

If two numbers are multiplied together to make 0,
one of the numbers must be 0.

Example: $7 \times \boxed{?} = 0$

↑

This number must be 0.

Remember: $(y + 2)(y - 4)$ means $(y + 2) \times (y - 4)$

If $(y + 2) \times (y - 4) = 0$

then either $y + 2 = 0$ **or** $y - 4 = 0$

$y = -2$ $y = 4$

Solving quadratic equations

If a question states:
"Solve $x^2 + 7x + 10 = 0$" it may factorise (see page 18).

But: If it says "Find x to any number of decimal places or significant figures", **or** If there is a number in front of x^2, eg $4x^2 + 7x + 10 = 0$, you **must** use the formula. This formula will be given on your exam paper.

For $ax^2 + bx + c = 0$

$$x = \frac{-b \pm \sqrt{b^2 - 4ac}}{2a}$$

Example

Solve $2x^2 - 12 = 7x$

First check you have
$$x^2 \text{ then } x \text{ then } \textbf{number} = \textbf{0}$$

If not, rearrange the equation:

$$2x^2 \quad - \quad 7x \quad - \quad 12 \quad = \quad 0$$

This is a   This is b   This is c
$a = 2$ $b = -7$ $c = -12$

Using the formula:

$$x = \frac{-b \pm \sqrt{b^2 - 4ac}}{2a}$$

$$x = \frac{--7 \pm \sqrt{(-7)^2 - (4 \times 2 \times -12)}}{2 \times 2}$$

$$x = \frac{7 \pm \sqrt{49 + 96}}{4}$$

$$x = \frac{7 \pm \sqrt{145}}{4}$$

$$x = \frac{7 + 12 \cdot 0415}{4} \quad \textbf{or} \quad x = \frac{7 - 12 \cdot 0415}{4}$$

$$x = 4 \cdot 76 \quad \textbf{or} \quad x = -1 \cdot 26$$

Questions

1. Solve $8x^2 + 32x + 15 = 0$

2. Solve $y^2 = 5y + 3$ correct to 3 significant figures

Answers

1. $a = 8$ $b = 32$ $c = 15$

$$x = \frac{-32 \pm \sqrt{32^2 - (4 \times 8 \times 15)}}{2 \times 8}$$

$$x = \frac{-32 \pm \sqrt{1024 - 480}}{16}$$

$$x = \frac{-32 \pm \sqrt{544}}{16}$$

$$x = \frac{-32 \pm 23 \cdot 3238}{16}$$

$$x = \frac{-32 + 23 \cdot 3238}{16} \quad \textbf{or} \quad x = \frac{-32 - 23 \cdot 3238}{16}$$

$$x = -0 \cdot 542 \quad \textbf{or} \quad x = -3 \cdot 46$$

2. First rearrange the equation:

$$y^2 \text{ then } y \text{ then } \textbf{number} = \textbf{0}$$

$$y^2 \quad - \quad 5y \quad - \quad 3 \quad = \quad 0$$

$a = 1$ $b = -5$ $c = -3$

$$x = \frac{--5 \pm \sqrt{(-5)^2 - (4 \times 1 \times -3)}}{2 \times 1}$$

Note: $y^2 = 1y^2$

$$x = \frac{5 \pm \sqrt{25 + 12}}{2}$$

$$x = \frac{5 \pm \sqrt{37}}{2}$$

$$x = \frac{5 \pm 6 \cdot 0827}{2}$$

$$x = \frac{5 + 6 \cdot 0827}{2} \quad \textbf{or} \quad x = \frac{5 - 6 \cdot 0827}{2}$$

$$x = 5 \cdot 54 \quad \textbf{or} \quad x = -0 \cdot 541$$

Simultaneous equations: Solving using algebra

I know there are quicker ways but here is a method for solving all simultaneous equations. I do not believe in lots of complicated rules and methods. This method will work every time in the same way.

Question

Solve the simultaneous equations: $4x - 5y = 2$
$3x - 2y = 5$

Answer

Make the numbers in front of the 'x' the same.

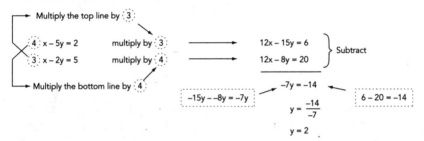

Substitute y = 2 into one of the original equations

$4x - 5y = 2$
$4x - 5 \times 2 = 2$
$4x - 10 = 2$
$4x = 2 + 10$
$4x = 12$
$x = 12 \div 4$
$x = 3$

Answer: x = 3, y = 2

Now check by substituting x = 3 and y = 2 in the other original equation
$3x - 2y = 5$
$3 \times 3 - 2 \times 2 = 5$
$9 - 4 = 5$

This is just a check. If you are short of time in an exam you can miss it out.

Sometimes the question is shown like this:

Solve the simultaneous equations $5x = 13 - 2y$ and $3y = 15 - 3x$

First write each question like this:

x terms		y terms	=	number
5x	+	2y	=	13
3x	+	3y	=	15

Now proceed as above.

Simplifying algebraic fractions – 1

You must look at indices (powers, page 15) and factorising (pages 17 to 19) before attempting these questions.

Simplifying

If you are asked to simplify you may need one of the methods shown in indices (powers), factorising or a method shown here.

Example 1   Simplify $\dfrac{6y - 8}{9y - 12}$

$\dfrac{6y - 8}{9y - 12}$ → 〔Factorise〕 → $\dfrac{2\cancel{(3y - 4)}}{3\cancel{(3y - 4)}}$ → 〔Cancel $(3y - 4)$〕 → $\dfrac{2}{3}$

Example 2   Simplify $\dfrac{x^2 - x - 6}{x^2 + 2x - 15}$

$\dfrac{x^2 - x - 6}{x^2 + 2x - 15}$ → 〔Factorise〕 → $\dfrac{(x + 2)\cancel{(x - 3)}}{(x + 5)\cancel{(x - 3)}}$ → 〔Cancel $(x - 3)$〕 → $\dfrac{(x + 2)}{(x + 5)}$

Example 3 Multiplication   Simplify $\dfrac{6a^2b}{5ab^2} \times \dfrac{4b^5}{9a}$

$\dfrac{6a^2b}{5ab^2} \times \dfrac{4b^5}{9a}$ → 〔multiply top and bottom lines〕 → $\dfrac{24a^2b^6}{45a^2b^2}$ → 〔Cancel (see above)〕 → $\dfrac{8b^4}{15}$

Example 4 Division   Simplify $\dfrac{6a^2b}{5ab^2} \div \dfrac{9a}{4b^5}$

$\dfrac{6a^2b}{5ab^2} \div \dfrac{9a}{4b^5}$ → 〔change ÷ sign to x〕 → 〔turn the fraction **after** the sign upside down〕 → $\dfrac{6a^2b}{5ab^2} \times \dfrac{4b^5}{9a}$

Now proceed in the same way as multiplication (example 3)

> **Multiplication and division are very similar**

Simplifying algebraic fractions – 2

Example 5 Addition

Simplify $\dfrac{5y}{6} + \dfrac{y-3}{4}$

$$\dfrac{5y}{6} + \dfrac{y-3}{4}$$

$$\dfrac{4\,(5y) \;+\; 6(y-3)}{6 \;\times\; 4}$$

multiply

$$\dfrac{20y + 6y - 18}{24}$$

$$\dfrac{26y - 18}{24}$$

$$\dfrac{2(13y - 9)}{24} \longrightarrow \boxed{\text{Cancel } \dfrac{2}{24}} \longrightarrow \dfrac{13y - 9}{12}$$

Example 6 Subtraction

Simplify $\dfrac{5y}{6} - \dfrac{y-3}{4}$

$$\dfrac{5y}{6} - \dfrac{y-3}{4}$$

$$\dfrac{4\,(5y) \;-\; 6(y-3)}{6 \;\times\; 4}$$

multiply

$$\dfrac{20y - 6y + 18}{24}$$

$$\dfrac{14y + 18}{24}$$

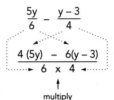

Common error:
Many candidates
put –18. This is wrong.
–6 x –3 = +18

$$\dfrac{2(7y + 9)}{24} \longrightarrow \boxed{\text{Cancel } \dfrac{2}{24}} \longrightarrow \dfrac{7y + 9}{12}$$

Addition and subtraction are very similar

Questions Simplify:

1. $\dfrac{10x - 15}{8x - 12}$

2. $\dfrac{8a^3b}{7ab^4} \div \dfrac{12a^2}{14ab}$

3. $\dfrac{3a}{5} - \dfrac{(4a + 5)}{8}$

Answers

1. $\dfrac{10x - 15}{8x - 12} \longrightarrow \boxed{\text{Factorise}} \longrightarrow \dfrac{5(2x - 3)}{4(2x - 3)} \longrightarrow \dfrac{5}{4}$

2. $\dfrac{8a^3b}{7ab^4} + \dfrac{12a^2}{14ab} \longrightarrow \boxed{\begin{array}{c}\text{Change} \div \text{ to x}\\ \text{Turn fraction after}\\ \text{sign upside down}\end{array}} \longrightarrow \dfrac{8a^3b}{7ab^4} \times \dfrac{14ab}{12a^2} \longrightarrow \boxed{\begin{array}{c}\text{Multiply top}\\ \text{and bottom lines}\end{array}} \longrightarrow \dfrac{112a^4b^2}{84a^3b^4}$

$\dfrac{112a^4b^2}{84a^3b^4} \longrightarrow \boxed{\text{Cancel}} \longrightarrow \dfrac{4a}{3b^2}$

Common error:
Many candidates put +25. This is wrong.
–5 x +5 = –25

3. $\dfrac{3a}{5} - \dfrac{(4a + 5)}{8} \longrightarrow \dfrac{8(3a) - 5(4a + 5)}{5 \times 8} \longrightarrow \dfrac{24a - 20a - 25}{40} \longrightarrow \dfrac{4a - 25}{40}$

Graphs

A big section with lots in it.

Drawing lines

Algebra and graphs are closely connected. You must be able to illustrate algebraic information in graphical form.

Graphical representation

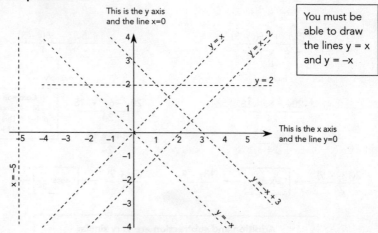

This is the y axis and the line x=0

$y = x$

$y = x - 2$

$y = 2$

This is the x axis and the line y=0

$x = -5$

$y = -x + 3$

$y = -x$

You must be able to draw the lines $y = x$ and $y = -x$

Question

Complete this table of values and draw the graph of $y = -x^2 + 4$

Note: Sometimes the question states draw the function $f(x) = -x^2 + 4$

x	–3	–2	–1	0	1	2	3
y							

Answer

If the question asks for the function $f(x) = -x^2 + 4$ the table and graph will be the same with $f(x)$ instead of y. When $x = -3$ $y = -(-3)^2 + 4 = -5$

x	–3	–2	–1	0	1	2	3
y	–5	0	3	4	3	0	–5

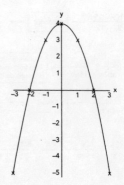

Simultaneous equations: Solving by drawing a graph

We solved simultaneous equations by calculation on page 21.
Now we see how to solve them by graphical methods.

Question

Solve the following pair of simultaneous equations by drawing a graph.

$y - 2x = 1$ and $2y - x = 8$

Answer

First draw $y - 2x = 1$

Choose three simple values of x:

eg When x = 0	When x = 1	When x = 3
$y - 2x = 1$	$y - 2x = 1$	$y - 2x = 1$
$y - 2 \times 0 = 1$	$y - 2 \times 1 = 1$	$y - 2 \times 3 = 1$
$y - 0 = 1$	$y - 2 = 1$	$y - 6 = 1$
$y = 1$	$y = 1 + 2$	$y = 1 + 6$
	$y = 3$	$y = 7$
(0,1)	(1,3)	(3,7)

Now draw $2y - x = 8$

Choose three simple values of x:

When x = 0	When x = 1	When x = 3
$2y - x = 8$	$2y - x = 8$	$2y - x = 8$
$2y - 0 = 8$	$2y - 1 = 8$	$2y - 3 = 8$
$2y = 8$	$2y = 8 + 1$	$2y = 8 + 3$
$y = {}^8/_2$	$2y = 9$	$2y = 11$
$y = 4$	$y = {}^9/_2$	$y = {}^{11}/_2$
	$y = 4.5$	$y = 5.5$
(0,4)	(1,4·5)	(3,5·5)

Plot the values on a graph.

Where the lines cross draw dotted lines.

The solution is $x = 2$, $y = 5$.

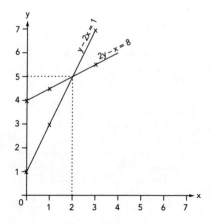

Solving equations using graphical methods

Equations can be solved in a variety of ways. One important method is by drawing a graph.

Example

Solve $x^2 + 2x = x + 3$

This is very similar to solving simultaneous equations by drawing a graph (page 25).

First draw $y = x^2 + 2x$.

Then draw $y = x + 3$.

The answer is where the two lines cross. Just read the x values.

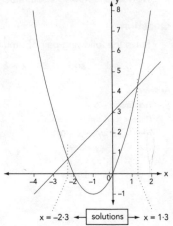

x	−4	−3	−2	−1	0	1	2
$x^2 + 2x$	8	3	0	−1	0	3	8
$x + 3$	−1	0	1	2	3	4	5

$x = -2.3$ ← solutions → $x = 1.3$

Questions

1 Solve $x^2 + 2x = 0$

2 Solve $x^2 + 2x = 5$

3 Use graphical methods to solve $x^2 + 3x = x + 4$ (use values of x between −4 and +2)

4 Draw $y = 2^x$ for $0 \le x \le 3$
   Use your graph to solve $2^x = 5$

Answers

1 $x^2 + 2x$ is drawn above. Draw the line $y = 0$ (ie the x axis). The solution is where this line crosses $y = x^2 + 2x$, ie $x = -2$ and $x = 0$

2 $x^2 + 2x$ is drawn above. Draw the line $y = 5$ (ie horizontal line at $y = 5$). Where the line crosses $y = x^2 + 2x$ is the solution, ie $x = 1.45$ and -3.45 (approx).

3 Draw graphs as shown in the example, ie draw $y = x^2 + 3x$ and $y = x + 4$.
   Answers $x = -3.2$ and 1.2 (approx.)

4

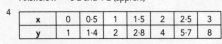

x	0	0·5	1	1·5	2	2·5	3
y	1	1·4	2	2·8	4	5·7	8

Method 2^x ⟶ $2^0 = 1$; $2^{0.5} = 1.4$; etc

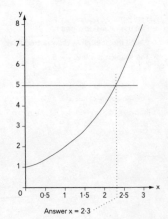

Answer $x = 2.3$

The straight line equation y = mx + c

We can find the equation of a straight line by calculating the gradient and where the line crosses the y-axis. You must learn 'y = mx + c'.

This is the gradient   This is where the line crosses the y axis

$$y = mx + c$$

$$m = \frac{\text{distance up}}{\text{distance across}}$$

If m is negative it is $\dfrac{\text{distance down}}{\text{distance across}}$

Examples

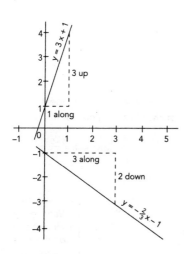

1 $y = 3x + 1$

       m   c

c = +1   means that the line crosses the y axis at +1

$$m = 3 = \frac{3}{1} \longrightarrow \frac{3 \text{ up the y axis}}{1 \text{ along the x axis}}$$

2 $y = -\frac{2}{3}x - 1$

       m   c

c = −1   means that the line crosses the y axis at −1

$$m = -\frac{2}{3} \longrightarrow \frac{2 \text{ down the y axis}}{3 \text{ along the x axis}}$$

Question

What is the equation of the line which passes through the points (1,2) and (3,1)?

Answer

Mark the points (1,2) and (3,1).
Draw a straight line through the points.

The equation of the line is
   y = mx + c
   m = −¹/₂
   c = 2·5
   y = −¹/₂ x + 2·5

The line slopes down
The gradient is −ve

Note:

If the line slopes up, the gradient (m) is positive.

If the line slopes down, the gradient (m) is negative.

27

Using tangents to find gradients

We can use tangents in a variety of situations, eg if we have a graph plotting time against distance, the gradient at any point will give the speed at that time (see *The straight line equation y = mx + c*, page 27).

Example Find the gradient of the curve at x = 25

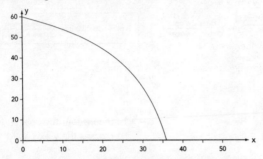

Place a ruler so that it touches but does not cut the curve. Draw a tangent.

This is a tangent. The tangent **touches** but does not cut the curve.

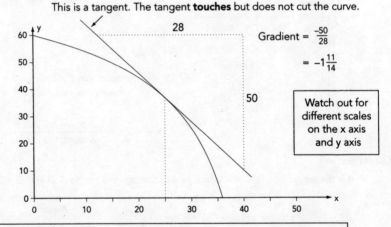

Gradient = $\frac{-50}{28}$

= $-1\frac{11}{14}$

> Watch out for different scales on the x axis and y axis

If the graphs shows time against distance, the gradient will be **speed**.
If the graphs shows time against speed, the gradient will be **acceleration**.

Questions

Draw the graph $y = -x^2 + 2$ for values $-3 < x < 3$

Find the gradient at: 1   x = -1   2   x = 0·5

Answers

1   2   2   -1

Expressing general rules in symbolic form – 1

Sometimes you will be given a table of values and asked to find the rule that connects the information.

This table shows the price of electricity:

Number of units used	50	100	150	200
Price (£)	9	13	17	21

a   Find a formula connecting price (P) and number of units (N) used

b   Use your formula to find the price when 4750 units are used

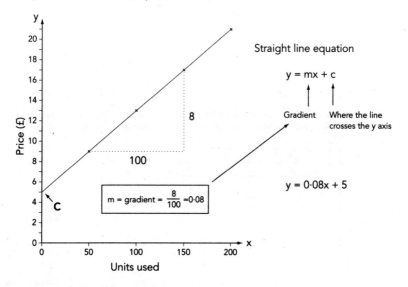

a $y = 0.08x + 5$ therefore   £P = £(0.08N + 5)

b   £P = £(0.08N + 5) = £(0.08 × 4750 + 5) = £385

Expressing general rules in symbolic form – 2

Questions

1   This table shows the price of hiring a car:

Distance (km)	10	20	30	40
Price (£)	23	26	29	32

    a   Find a formula connecting price (P) and distance (D)

    b   Calculate the cost for a distance of 120 km

2   Two variables x and y are connected by the equation $y = ax^2 + b$.
Here are some values of x and y:

x	2	4	5
y	4	10	14·5

Find the value of a and b

Answers

1   a   £P = £(0·3D + 20)   b   £P = £(0·3 x 120 + 20) = £56

2   If we plot a graph of y against x we will get a curve. To find the connection we must have a straight line.
Therefore we plot a graph of y against x^2 (**Note**: the question told us y was connected to x^2)

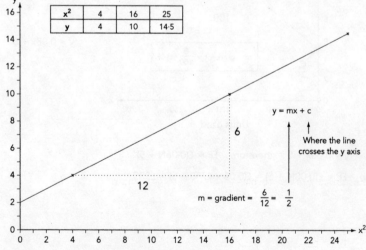

x^2	4	16	25
y	4	10	14·5

This gives $y = \frac{1}{2}x + 2$ but we plotted y against x^2 not x

Therefore the equation of the line is $y = \frac{1}{2}x^2 + 2$.

The question states $y = ax^2 + b$. $a = \frac{1}{2}$ b = 2

Drawing graphs

No shortcuts here. You simply have to memorise what the graphs look like.

Graphs

You should recognise these graphs.

Linear graphs   such as $y = 3x + 6$, $y = -\frac{1}{2}x + 2$, etc

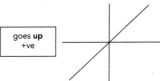

y = x

y = −x

goes **up**
+ve

goes **down**
−ve

Quadratic graphs such as $y = 2x^2 + 3x - 6$, $y = -3x^2 + x + 4$, etc

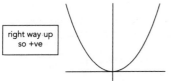

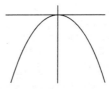

$y = x^2$

$y = -x^2$

right way up
so +ve

upside
down so −ve

Cubic graphs such as $y = x^3 + 2x^2 + x - 1$, $y = -3x^3 + x^2 - 4$, etc

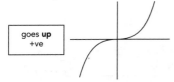

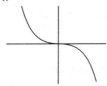

$y = x^3$

$y = -x^3$

goes **up**
+ve

goes **down**
−ve

Reciprocal graphs such as $y = \frac{3}{2x}$, $y = \frac{-4}{x}$, etc

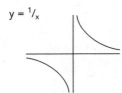

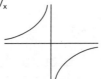

$y = \frac{1}{x}$

$y = -\frac{1}{x}$

Sketching graphs – 1

It is useful to be able to look at a function and recognise its general appearance and characteristics without plotting exact points.

f(x) is a function of x

eg f(x) = 2x – 1, f(x) = 4x^2 – 2, f(x) = cos x

We draw the function f(x) = 2x – 1 in the same way as y = 2x – 1.

The exam question usually has a function drawn and you have to draw the new function.

Here are the rules. It is a good idea to learn them.

Suppose f(x) is drawn on the exam paper, the question will ask you to draw one of these:

y = f(x) + a	eg y = f(x) + 2 means move f(x) 2 units **up** [ie add 2 to every y co-ordinate, so (4,6) becomes (4,8)] See Figure 1

y = f(x) – a	eg y = f(x) – 2 means move f(x) 2 units **down** [ie subtract 2 from every y co-ordinate, so (4,6) becomes (4,4)] See Figure 1

y = f(x – a)	eg y = f(x – 2) means move f(x) 2 units **right** [ie add 2 to every x co-ordinate, so (4,6) becomes (6,6)] See Figure 1

y = f(x + a)	eg y = f(x + 2) means move f(x) 2 units **left** [ie subtract 2 from every x co-ordinate, so (4,6) becomes (2,6)] See Figure1

These do the opposite of what you would expect

y = f(ax)	eg y = f(2x) means **divide** every x co-ordinate by 2 [so (4,3) becomes (2,3)]. See Figure 2 **Note:** y = f(^{x}/₂) means y = f(^{1}/₂x). Therefore divide every x co-ordinate by ^{1}/₂, eg (4,6) becomes (8,6)

y = af(x)	eg y = 2f(x) means **multiply** every y co-ordinate by 2 [so (4,3) becomes (4,6)]. See Figure 3 **Note:** y = –f(x) means y = –1f(x). Therefore multiply every y co-ordinate by –1, eg (4,6) becomes (4,–6.)

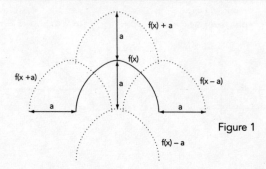

Figure 1

Sketching graphs – 2

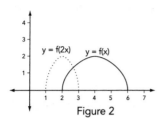

Figure 2

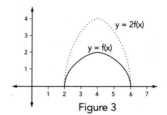

Figure 3

Questions

1   This is a graph of y = f(x)

    a   Draw the graph of y = f(x) + 1

    b   Draw the graph of y = f(x – 1)

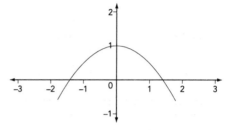

2   This is a graph of y = sin(x)

    a   Draw the graph of y = 2sin(x)

    b   Draw the graph of y = sin(2x)

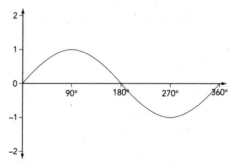

Answers

1   y = f(x) + 1   move graph 1 **up**

      y = f(x – 1)   move graph 1 **right**

2   y = 2sin(x)   multiply every y co-ordinate by 2

      y = sin(2x)   divide every x co-ordinate by 2

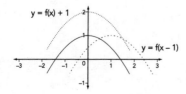

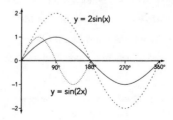

Speed, time and distance graphs

You will be asked to read information from graphs.

This graph shows the journey made
by a car. What is the speed at 0900?

Note: The question may use the
word velocity instead of speed.

> **Note:**
> The gradient gives
> the speed or velocity

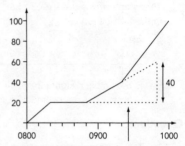

Answer:
Speed = 40 km/h

Make this line exactly one hour. Form a right-angled triangle (dotted lines).
The height of the triangle will be the speed in kilometres per hour.

Questions

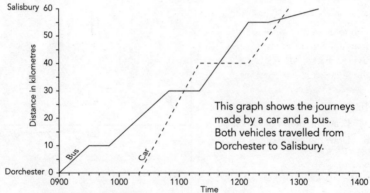

This graph shows the journeys
made by a car and a bus.
Both vehicles travelled from
Dorchester to Salisbury.

1 a Between which times did the bus travel fastest?
   b How did you decide?

2 Describe what happened at 11·40.

3 How many times did the car pass the bus?

4 How long did the car stop for?

5 What was the speed of the bus on the first part of its journey?

6 What was the speed of the car at 12·30?

Answers

1 a 11:20 and 12:10   b The steeper the graph, the faster the bus

2 The bus passed the car   3 twice   4 50 minutes

5 20 km/h   6 30 km/h

Area under a curve

Example

This graph shows the speed of a plane
in the first 8 seconds.

a   Estimate the total distance travelled
    by dividing the area under the curve
    into four trapezia.

b   Is the actual distance travelled more
    or less than your estimate? Explain why.

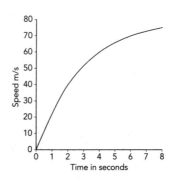

Method

The area under the curve represents
the distance travelled.

a   The total distance is

    40 m + 100 m + 130 m + 145 m = 415 m

b   The total area of the trapezia is less
    than the area under the curve. Therefore
    the estimate of 415 m is slightly less than
    the actual distance travelled.

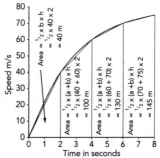

Question

This curve shows the
speed of a motor cycle
during a period of
12 seconds. Estimate
the total distance
travelled by using
three trapezia.

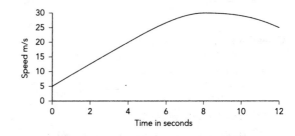

Answer

The total distance is

50 m + 100 m + 110 m = 260 m

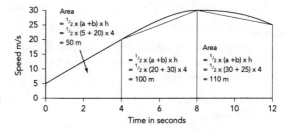

Angles

You will need to use this information later when you work with circles.

Intersecting and parallel lines

You need to know the following information about angles. You often need to extend lines to make Z shapes. If you are used to seeing parallel lines going across the page and a question has the lines going down the page it can sometimes help to turn the paper around.

Intersecting lines

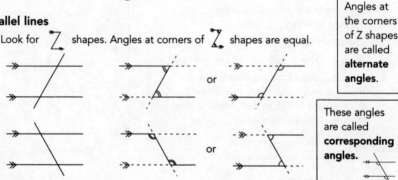

$a + b = 180°$
$b + c = 180°$
$c + d = 180°$ } Angles on a straight line add up to 180°
$d + a = 180°$

$a = c$
$b = d$ } Vertically opposite angles are equal

Parallel lines

Look for ⟍ shapes. Angles at corners of ⟍ shapes are equal.

or

or

> Angles at the corners of Z shapes are called **alternate angles**.

> These angles are called **corresponding angles**.

Questions

1   Find the missing angles:

2   Find x: 3   Find y:

Answers

1   a = 140°, b = 40°, c = 140°, d = 40°, e = 140°, f = 40°, g = 140°.

2   It often helps to extend the parallel lines to produce Z shapes.

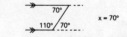

x = 70°

3   Try adding an extra parallel line

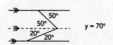

y = 70°

36

Bearings

Bearings are measured clockwise from North. They are easier to measure with a circular protractor (diameter 10 cm). North will usually be shown as vertically up the page. Ensure the 0° on the protractor is on the North line. REMEMBER if the question states "measure the bearing of C from D" you put your protractor on D. Put your protractor on the "from" part of the question.

Questions

1   What is the bearing of A from B?

2   What is the bearing of B from A?

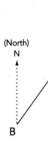

Note: If you know the bearing from A to B, then the bearing from B to A will be 180° more or 180° less, eg:

037° + 180° = 217°
217° − 180° = 037°

Answers

1   Bearings are always measured clockwise from North.
   Place your protractor on B. Measure the angle between north and AB.
   The angle is 37°.
   Bearings are always written as three figures. Answer = 037°

2   Place your protractor on A. Measure the angle. The angle is 217°.
   Answer 217°

Similarity

This usually appears on the exam paper. Just recognise the shapes, put them the same way round, then find the scale factor (ie the relationship between the sizes of the shapes).

Similarity

An easy method is shown below.

Two triangles are similar if the angles of one triangle are equal to the angles of the other triangle, eg:

 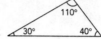

Question

Find the length of AB and AE.

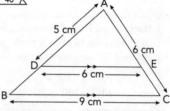

Answer

DE is parallel to BC. Therefore ADE is similar to ABC.

1 Draw the two triangles separately.

2 Identify the big triangle and the small triangle.

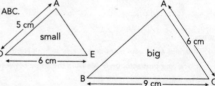

3 Find two sides with lengths given which are in the same position on each triangle. In this example DE and BC.
   DE = 6 cm,   BC = 9 cm

4 The scale factor (SF) from small to big is $\frac{9}{6}$ ie $\frac{big}{small}$.
   To convert any length on the small triangle to a length on the large triangle, multiply by SF $\frac{9}{6}$.
   eg   AD (small triangle) x SF $\frac{9}{6}$ = AB
        5 cm x $\frac{9}{6}$ = 7·5 cm

5 The scale factor from big to small is $\frac{6}{9}$ ie $\frac{small}{big}$.
   To convert any length on the large triangle to a length on the small triangle, multiply by SF $\frac{6}{9}$.
   eg AC (large triangle) x SF $\frac{6}{9}$ = AE
       6 cm x $\frac{6}{9}$ = 4 cm

Congruency

If two shapes are congruent they are identical. The angles of one shape are equal to the angles of the other shape **and** the sides of one shape are equal to the sides of the other shape.

Congruent triangles – 1

You must be able to identify congruent triangles.

> **Congruent** means exactly the same shape and size

When you test for congruency you may have to turn one of the triangles or flip one over.

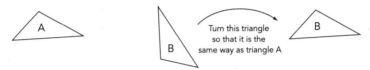

Turn this triangle so that it is the same way as triangle A

If two triangles obey any of the following tests they are congruent.

Tests for congruent triangles (A=Angle, S=Side, R=Right angle, H=Hypotenuse.)

> Memorise: **SSS**   **SAS**   **AAS**   **RHS**

A **common error** is to think AAA is a test for congruency. It is NOT.

But it is a test for similarity (see page 38).

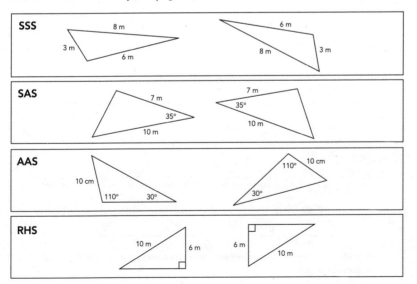

Congruent triangles – 2

Questions

Decide which of the following triangles are congruent.

If they are congruent give a reason, eg SAS.

1   **2**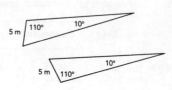

3 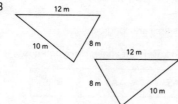   **4**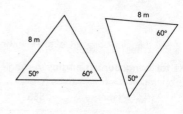

5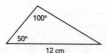

Answers

1 Not congruent (AAA is not a test for congruency)
2 Congruent AAS
3 Congruent SSS
4 Not congruent. In one triangle 8 is opposite 60°, in the other it is opposite 50°.
5 This is one of the examiner's favourites. At first glance it appears the triangles are not congruent.

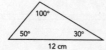

Advice: Wherever you have a triangle with two angles always add the third angle to the diagram

Congruent ASA or AAS

Transformations

There are four types of transformation (you may be asked to describe a transformation).

1 Translation   describe using a vector eg $\begin{pmatrix} 4 \\ -2 \end{pmatrix}$ means 4 right, 2 down

2 Reflection   you must state where the mirror line is

3 Rotation   state: a   centre of rotation
                                b   angle of rotation
                                c   clockwise or anticlockwise

4 Enlargement   state: a   scale factor
                                b   centre of enlargement

Combined and inverse transformations

Combined transformations

This means two or more transformations, eg a shape could be enlarged and then reflected.

Inverse transformations

The exam question will tell you how to move shape A to shape B. The inverse operation is moving shape B back to shape A, ie the opposite.

1 **Translation:** A shape R is translated by the vector $\begin{pmatrix} a \\ b \end{pmatrix}$ to produce R'. The inverse to take R' back to R is $\begin{pmatrix} -a \\ -b \end{pmatrix}$.

2 **Reflection:** A shape R is reflected in the line y = x to produce R'. The inverse to take R' back to R is reflection in the line y = x

3 **Rotation:** A shape R is rotated through an angle of 90° clockwise, centre of rotation the point (5, 2) to produce R'. The inverse to take R' back to R is rotation through an angle of 90° anticlockwise, centre of rotation the point (5, 2).

4 **Enlargement:** A shape R is enlarged by a scale factor of $^3/_4$, centre of enlargement the point (5, 1) to produce R'. The inverse to take R' back to R is enlarge by a scale factor of $^4/_3$, centre of enlargement the point (5, 1)

Questions

1 A shape C is translated by the vector $\begin{pmatrix} -3 \\ 5 \end{pmatrix}$ to produce shape D.

   Describe the transformation to return shape D to C.

2 A shape T is rotated through an angle of 270° anticlockwise, centre of rotation the point (1, –4) to produce T'. Describe the transformation to return T' to T.

Answers

1 Translation by the vector $\begin{pmatrix} 3 \\ -5 \end{pmatrix}$

2 Rotation through an angle of 270° clockwise (or 90° anticlockwise), centre of rotation the point (1,–4).

Enlargement by a fractional scale factor

Note: Enlargement by a scale factor less than 1 makes the shape **smaller**.

Question

Enlarge the triangle by a scale factor of $^2/_3$. Centre of enlargement is the point (1,1).

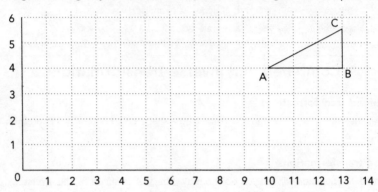

Answer

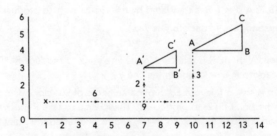

Count the distance from the centre of enlargement to each point.

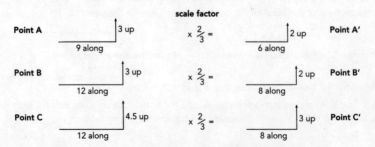

Note: Always count from the centre of enlargement.
A common error is to count from the origin, ie the point (0, 0).

Enlargement by a negative scale factor

Note: The method is almost identical to enlargement by a fractional scale factor (see page 42).

Question

A triangle has co-ordinates A (8, 4), B (11, 6), C (11, 4).

Enlarge the triangle by a scale factor of –3, centre of enlargement the point (5, 2). Label the enlargement A'B'C'. What are the co-ordinates of the new triangle?

Answer

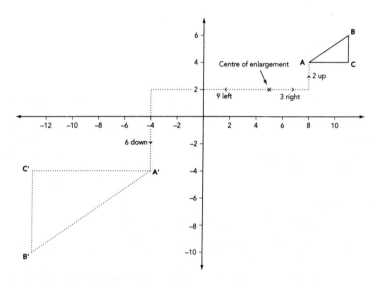

Count the distance from the centre of enlargement to each point.

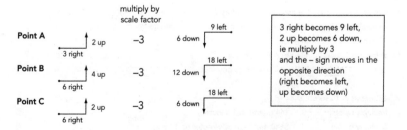

A common error is to count from the origin (0, 0).
Remember: Always count from the centre of enlargement

Measurement

Quite a lot to memorise if you don't already know it. Most of this section is everyday Maths. Nothing difficult.

Compound measures

Speed and density are compound measures because we give the speed in m/s or km/h, ie two units. If mass is given in kg and volume in m^3, the density will be given in kg/m^3.

The following formulae must be memorised:

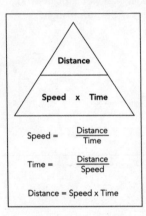

Speed = $\dfrac{Distance}{Time}$

Time = $\dfrac{Distance}{Speed}$

Distance = Speed x Time

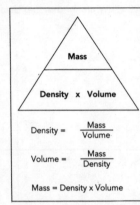

Density = $\dfrac{Mass}{Volume}$

Volume = $\dfrac{Mass}{Density}$

Mass = Density x Volume

You may have used these formulae in Science.

Suppose you want to know what speed equals. Cover up speed. This shows:

Therefore Speed = $\dfrac{Distance}{Time}$

You will use this method in trigonometry (that is sin, cos, tan) on page 59.

Questions

1   A car takes 8 hours 10 minutes to travel 343 kilometres. Calculate the average speed.

2   A man walks at a speed of 24 metres in 10 seconds. Calculate his speed in kilometres per hour.

3   Mass is given in g, volume is given in cm^3. What units are used for density?

Answers

1   Decide if you require the answer in kilometres per hour or kilometres per minute.

If you choose kilometres per hour change 8 hours 10 minutes into hours.

10 minutes is $^{10}/_{60}$ of an hour.

Therefore 8 hours 10 minutes = $8^{10}/_{60}$ hours.

Speed = $\dfrac{Distance}{Time}$ = $\dfrac{343}{8^{10}/_{60}}$ = 42 kilometres per hour.

2   24 metres in 10 seconds

(multiply by 6)	144 metres in 1 minute
(multiply by 60)	8640 metres in 60 minutes (ie 1 hour)
(divide by 1000)	8.64 kilometres in 1 hour
	The speed is 8.64 kilometres per hour.

3   g/cm^3

Time

Your examination paper may contain a time question. We use time frequently so it should be easy. WARNING: At least half of the examination candidates will get the question wrong. Treat the question with respect. Remember there are 60 minutes in an hour NOT 10 or 100; lots of candidates will make this mistake.

A common error is to think 3·5 hours equals 3 hours 50 minutes. It does not. It equals 3 hours 30 minutes. Your calculator will change hours (as a decimal) into hours, minutes and seconds. (**Note:** You can only use this method if your calculator has these keys.)

Find the [D°M'S"] key or [○ ' "] or [" "] .

These are very useful keys.

Put 3·5 into your calculator and press the [D°M'S"] key or you may have to press the top left key on your calculator (ie [shift] or [INV] or [2nd] followed by [○ ' "] or [" "]).

You should get 3°30'00·00 or 3°30'0 this means 3 hours 30 minutes.

Questions

1 A train leaves London at 07:42 and arrives in Glasgow at 13:16. How long does the journey take?

2 A car travels 378 km at 67·9 km/h. How long does the journey take? Give your answer to the nearest second.

You must know:

60 seconds = 1 minute
60 minutes = 1 hour
24 hours = 1 day
365 days = 1 year

Answers

1 If you have 5 hours 34 minutes, stick with your own method.

If you obtained the answer 5 hours 74 minutes or 6 hours 14 minutes you have fallen straight into the trap and must study the solution carefully.

		Hours	Minutes
First find the time to the next whole hour.	07:42 to 08:00		18
Now the hours	08:00 to 13:00	5	
Now the minutes	13:00 to 13:16		16
		5 hours	34 minutes

2 Time = $\dfrac{\text{Distance}}{\text{Speed}}$ (see page 44).

$\dfrac{378}{67·9}$ = 5·567010309 **Note:** This does **not** mean 5 hours 56 minutes or 5 hours 57 minutes. Use the [D°M'S"] or [" "] key to change your answer = 5 hours 34 minutes 1 second.

Measurement

Upper and lower bounds of numbers – 1

Some numbers can be written exactly, eg 3 girls (you cannot have 3·72 girls). Some numbers, particularly measures, have a degree of accuracy, eg a height may be given as 172 cm, correct to the nearest centimetre. This means that the height is 172 cm± 0·5 cm, ie between 171·5 cm and 172·5 cm.

Finding the upper and lower bounds of numbers means calculating the maximum and minimum possible values. You need to know how to do easy questions first.

Example

5·72 is correct to two decimal places. Find:

a   the maximum possible value   b   the minimum possible value

Method

5·72 is correct to two decimal places, ie correct to 0·01.
The error can be half of this, ie 0·005

a   maximum = 5·72 + 0·005 = 5·725   b   minimum = 5·72 – 0·005 = 5·715

Question

A, B, C and D are measured correct to one decimal place:

A 5·3, B 4·2, C 3·8, D 1·7.

Calculate the upper and lower bounds for $(A + B) - \dfrac{C}{D}$

Answer

First find the maximum and minimum values of A, B, C and D

$A = 5·3 < \begin{matrix} 5·35 \text{ (max)} \\ 5·25 \text{ (min)} \end{matrix}$ $B = 4·2 < \begin{matrix} 4·25 \text{ (max)} \\ 4·15 \text{ (min)} \end{matrix}$ $C = 3·8 < \begin{matrix} 3·85 \text{ (max)} \\ 3·75 \text{ (min)} \end{matrix}$ $D = 1·7 < \begin{matrix} 1·75 \text{ (max)} \\ 1·65 \text{ (min)} \end{matrix}$

There are several complicated rules for finding minimum and maximum values.
When you **add** or **multiply** it is **obvious**.

Addition	to find max	maximum + maximum
	to find min	minimum + minimum
Multiplication	to find max	maximum x maximum
	to find min	minimum x minimum

Be careful if you are using negative numbers.

When you **subtract** or **divide** strange things happen.

Subtraction	to find max	maximum – minimum
	to find min	minimum – maximum
Division	to find max	maximum ÷ minimum
	to find min	minimum ÷ maximum

Be careful if you are using negative numbers.

You can either learn these rules or work it out in the exam.

Upper and lower bounds of numbers – 2

> If you work it out just remember:
>
> addition and multiplication are **obvious** (unless there are negative numbers)
> with subtraction and division **strange things happen**

Advice: Work out each part separately.

First A + B **obvious**

maximum of A + B = maximum + maximum
= 5·35 + 4·25
= 9·6

minimum of A + B = minimum + minimum
= 5·25 + 4·15
= 9·4

Now $\dfrac{C}{D}$ **strange things happen**

Either use the rules or work it out. If you work it out, there are four possibilities.
The best way is to try out all four **but** it is usually min/max or max/min.

$\dfrac{\text{max}}{\text{max}}$ ⟶ $\dfrac{3·85}{1·75}$ = 2·2   **no use**

$\dfrac{\text{max}}{\text{min}}$ ⟶ $\dfrac{3·85}{1·65}$ = 2·3333...   **maximum**

$\dfrac{\text{min}}{\text{max}}$ ⟶ $\dfrac{3·75}{1·75}$ = 2·142857..   **minimum**

$\dfrac{\text{min}}{\text{min}}$ ⟶ $\dfrac{3·75}{1·65}$ = 2·272727..   **no use**

Now   (A + B) $<$ 9·6 (max) / 9·4 (min) $\dfrac{C}{D}$ $<$ 2·333333.. (max) / 2·142857.. (min)

(A + B) – $\dfrac{C}{D}$ subtraction **strange things happen**

There are four possibilities – try each:

max – max ⟶ 9·6 – 2·333333 = 7·266667
max – min ⟶ 9·6 – 2·142857 = 7·457143 ⟶ **maximum**
min – max ⟶ 9·4 – 2·333333 = 7·066667 ⟶ **minimum**
min – min ⟶ 9·4 – 2·142857 = 7·257143

Circles

You are advised to memorise the formulae for circles.

Length, area and volume of shapes with curves

To find the area of the sector

First find the area of the circle

Then $\dfrac{y°}{360°}$ x area

To find the length of the arc

First find the circumference of the circle

Then $\dfrac{y°}{360°}$ x circumference

> **Remember:** All you have to do is multiply by
> $$\dfrac{\text{angle at the centre of the circle}}{360°}$$

You will be asked to use these formulae. They will be given on the exam paper (no need to memorise them).

The following questions show you what you are expected to do.

Surface area of a sphere:	$4\pi r^2$
Volume of a sphere:	$\frac{4}{3}\pi r^3$
Volume of a cone:	$\pi r^2 h$
Curved surface area of a cone:	π x base radius x slant height

Questions

1. Find a   the area of the sector OAB
   b   the length of the arc AB

2. Find the shaded area. **Note:** The shaded area is a segment.
3. The volume of a sphere is 80 cm². Find the radius.
4. Find the total surface area of a cylinder, radius 4 cm, height 6 cm.

Answers

1. a   Area of a circle = $\pi r^2 = \pi \times 8^2 = 201$ cm²
   Area of sector = $\frac{40}{360} \times 201 = 22\cdot3$ cm²

   b   Circumference of a circle = $2\pi r = 2 \times \pi \times 8 = 50\cdot3$ cm
   Length of arc $= \frac{40}{360} \times 50\cdot3 = 5\cdot59$ cm

2. **First**, find the area of sector OCD.
   Area of circle = $\pi r^2 = \pi \times 5^2 = 78\cdot5398$ cm²
   area of sector OCD $= \frac{60}{360} \times 78\cdot5398$
   $= 13\cdot089969$ cm²

   Second, find the area of triangle OCD.
   (OC and OD are radii therefore OC = OD = 5 cm)
   Area of a triangle $= \frac{1}{2} ab \sin c$
   $= \frac{1}{2} \times 5 \times 5 \times \sin 60°$
   $= 10\cdot825318$ cm²

   Third, area of sector – area of triangle = shaded area = $13\cdot089969 - 10\cdot825318 = 2\cdot26$ cm²

3. Volume of a sphere $= \frac{4}{3}\pi r^3$
   $80 = \frac{4}{3}\pi r^3$
   $\dfrac{80}{\frac{4}{3}\pi} = r^3$
   $19\cdot09859 = r^3$
   $\sqrt[3]{19\cdot09859} = r = 2\cdot67$ cm

4. Area of the curved sector is:
   $2\pi rh = 2 \times \pi \times 4 \times 6 = 150\cdot796$ cm²
   plus area of the circles:
   $2 \times \pi r^2 = 2 \times \pi \times 4^2 = 100\cdot531$ cm²
   total area = $150\cdot8 + 100\cdot5 = 251$ cm²

Angle and tangent properties of circles – 1

We have **three** rules for circles and **three** rules for tangents. You **must** memorise them.

Angle rule 1

The angle at the centre of a circle is twice the angle at the circumference.
This can appear on the examination paper in different ways (O is the centre).
Actually they are all the same, they just look different.

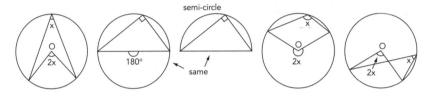

Angle rule 2

Look at the **equal** angles.

Angle rule 3

Cyclic quadrilateral
A 4-sided shape inside a circle.
All 4 vertices lie on the
circumference of the circle

Remember:
Opposite angles
add up to 180°,
ie $a + c = b + d = 180°$

Radius

This is an examiners' favourite which is often missed by candidates.

O is the centre
OA is a radius
OB is a radius
Therefore OA = OB, ie OAB is an isosceles triangle
and angle A = angle B

You also need to know the obvious

1 Angles in a triangle add up to 180°
2 Angles on a straight line add up to 180°
3 Angles at a point add up to 360°
4 Parallel lines mean Z shapes (see page 36)

Angle and tangent properties of circles – 2

A tangent is a line which just touches but does not cut a circle.

Tangent rule 1

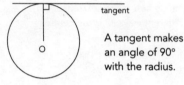

A tangent makes an angle of 90° with the radius.

Tangent rule 2

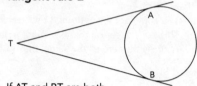

If AT and BT are both tangents to this circle then AT = BT

If we combine rules 1 and 2:

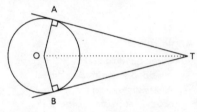

Triangles ATO and BTO are congruent.

Tangent rule 3

angle BTD = angle TCD
angle ATC = angle TDC

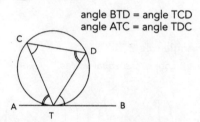

This one doesn't come up very often, but if it does most candidates will miss it.

That's it for circles. It **must** be one of these rules (but don't forget the **obvious**). The easiest way to work out the size of angles is to:

1   Draw a large diagram.

2   Forget what the question asks you to find. Instead fill in all the angles you can work out easily. If you are certain, fill in the angle on your diagram in pen. If you are not certain use pencil.

3   Do **not** forget the **obvious.**

4   Turn your diagram around. Things can look different from other directions.

5   Look for the **three** rules for circles. If there are tangents look for the **three** rules of tangents. If this does not help it must be something **obvious**.

Angle and tangent properties of circles – 3

Questions

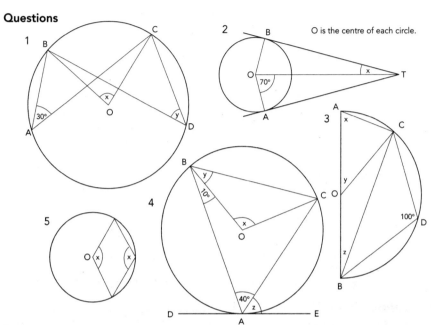

O is the centre of each circle.

Answers

1   To find x

This is an example of angle rule 1. It is easier to see if you turn the question upside down. Answer x = 60°

To find y

This is an example of angle rule 2. Answer y = 30°

4   To find x

This may be easier if you turn it upside down. Use angle rule 1 Answer x = 80°

To find y

OB is a radius } It is easy to
OC is a radius } miss this
Therefore triangle OBC is isosceles
Angle OBC = angle OCB
Answer y = 50°

To find z

This is an example of tangent rule 3. Answer z = 60°

2   To find x

Triangle ATO is congruent to triangle BTO. Therefore angle TOA = angle TOB = 70°. Angle TBO = 90° (see tangent rule 1). Now use the obvious, ie angles in a triangle = 180° Answer x = 20°

5   This is an example of angle rule 1

2x + x = 360°
(angles at a point = 360°)
3x = 360°
x = 120°

3   This may be easier if you turn the question (90° anticlockwise) and imagine a complete circle.

To find x

This is an example of angle rule 3. ABCD is a cyclic quadrilateral. Answer x = 80°

To find y

OA is a radius } It is easy to
OC is a radius } miss this
Therefore triangle OAC is isosceles
Angle ACO is 80°
Answer y = 20°

To find z

Either
Angle ACB = 90° (angle rule 1)
Therefore z = 10°
or
Angle AOC is twice ABC (angle rule 1)
Angle AOC = 20° therefore
angle ABC = 10°   Answer z = 10°

Perimeter, area and volume

Fairly straightforward. They give you the formulae on the exam paper so that makes it easier.

Calculating length, area and volume – 1

You need to understand length, area, volume, perimeter and know the units each is measured in. You must know what is meant by cross-section, prism, parallelogram, trapezium, and how to use the formulae. (These formulae will be given on the examination paper.)

> **Remember:** Perimeter is the distance around a shape.
> Area is measured in units^2, eg mm^2, cm^2, m^2
> Volume is measured in units^3, eg mm^3, cm^3, m^3

You are expected to know how to use these formulae:

Area of a triangle
= $^1/_2$ x base x perpendicular height (P.H.)

Area of a parallelogram
= base x perpendicular height

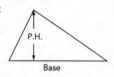

Area of a trapezium
= $^1/_2$ (a + b) x perpendicular height

Volume of a cuboid
= length x width x height

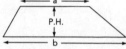

Questions

1 Find a the perimeter; and
     b the area of this shape.

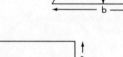

2 Find the area.

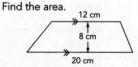

3 Find the area.

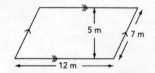

4 Find the area.

5 Find the volume.

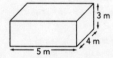

Answers

1   a   8 cm + 3 cm + 8 cm + 3 cm = 22 cm   b   8 cm x 3 cm = 24 cm^2

2   $^1/_2$ x 7 cm x 6 cm = 21 cm^2 3   12 m x 5 m = 60 m^2 (**Note:** 7m is not used)

4   Area = $^1/_2$ x (12 cm + 20 cm) x 8 cm   5   5 m x 4 m x 3 m = 60 m^3

            = $^1/_2$ x 32 cm   x 8 cm

            = 128 cm^2 (**Common error:** 128 cm^2 does **not** equal 1·28 m^2 – see page 56)

Calculating length, area and volume – 2

Prism

Any solid shape with uniform cross-section, ie same shape at each end.

Cross-section

This is the shape that goes all through a prism, ie the shaded parts in these shapes.

Example

Find the volume of this prism:

Volume = cross–sectional area x length

First find the cross–sectional area

Area of a triangle = $^1/_2$ base x height = $^1/_2$ x 5 x 3 = 7·5 cm^2

Note: The length is 1·5 m. This must be changed into centimetres, ie 150 cm.

Volume = 7·5 cm^2 x 150 cm = 1125 cm^3

Question

Find the area and perimeter of this shape:

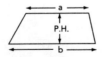

Answer

The formula to find the area of a trapezium is $^1/_2$ (a+b) x perpendicular height.

Area = $^1/_2$ (4 + 10) x 6

      = $^1/_2$ (14) x 6

      = 7 x 6

      = 42 cm^2

To find the perimeter we must use Pythagoras' theorem to find the missing side (see *Pythagoras' theorem, page 57*).

$x^2 = 6^2 + 6^2$

$x^2 = 36 + 36$

$x^2 = 72$

$x = \sqrt{72}$

$x = 8.49$ cm

Perimeter = 4 + 6 + 10 + 8.49 = 28.49 cm

Calculating length, area and volume – 3

Questions

1 a Find the area.
  b Find the perimeter.

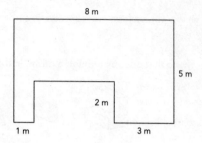

2 This is a diagram of a garden with a lawn and a path around the edge. The path is 2 m wide.

   Find the area of the path.

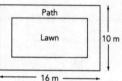

3 Find the volume of this cuboid.

Answers

1 a Split the shape into three parts.
     Area = 32 m²
  b 8 m + 5 m + 3 m + 2 m
     + 4 m + 2 m + 1 m + 5 m = 30 m

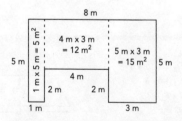

2 Find the area of the large rectangle = 10 x 16   = 160 m²
  Find the area of the small rectangle = 6 x 12   = 72 m²
  Take away   = 88 m²

   Note: It is 6 x 12
   A common error is 8 x 14.
   Remember 2 m wide at both ends

3 Be careful with this. Note the units. Either change everything to metres or everything to centimetres.
   Answer 168 000 cm³ or 0·168m³

Formulae for length, area and volume

You need to recognise formulae. Which ones are 1-D (length), 2-D (area) and 3-D (volume)?

Length has 1 dimension
Area has 2 dimensions
Volume has 3 dimensions

Length x length = area
Length x length x length = volume
Length x area = volume

Length + length = length
Area + area = area
Volume + volume = volume

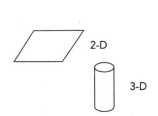

1-D

2-D

3-D

Different dimensions cannot be added. For example:

Length cannot be added to area
Volume cannot be added to area
Length cannot be added to volume

Numbers, eg 3, 7, π have no effect on the dimensions. They are just numbers.
For example:

r = radius
r is a length
r^2 is an area

$2\pi r$ is a length
πr^2 is an area

> **Note:** Perimeter, radius and diameter are all lengths

Questions

a, b, c and d are lengths.

State whether each formula gives a length, area, volume or none of these.

1   3ab

2   $\dfrac{bcd}{3a}$

3   $ab^2 + 3cd^2$

4   ab + d

Answers

1   length x length = area
    Answer area

2   $\dfrac{bcd}{3a}$ = $\dfrac{length \times length \times length}{length}$ = $\dfrac{volume}{length}$
    Answer area

3   $\qquad ab^2 + 3cd^2$
    length x length x length + length x length x length
    $\qquad$ volume + volume

    Answer volume

4   $\qquad ab + d$
    length x length + length
    $\qquad$ area + length

    area cannot be added to length
    Answer none of these

55

Ratio for length, area and volume

Look at this

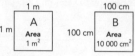

The two squares are identical.
The area of A is 1 m². The area of B is 10 000 cm².

Note: Common error, 1 m²
does not equal 100 cm².
Be very careful when converting
units of area and volume.

Let us see why this happens

side 2 cm   side 3 cm

Ratio of sides (length)	x : y	ie 2 : 3
Ratio of areas	x² : y²	ie 2² : 3² → 4 : 9
Ratio of volumes	x³ : y³	ie 2³ : 3³ → 8 : 27

Note: If you are given the area ratio you can find the length ratio by taking the square root.
If you are given the volume ratio you can find the length ratio by taking the cube root.

Example

A map is drawn to a scale of 4 cm represents 10 km.
The area of a lake on the map is 20 cm². What is the area of the real lake?

Length ratio is   4 cm : 10 km
Area ratio is   (4 cm)² : (10 km)² → 16 cm² : 100 km²
(divide by 16 to find 1 cm³)   1 cm² : 6.25 km²
                  20 cm² : 125 km²   Answer 125 km²

or you could use the scale factor method ie 20 x (¹⁰/₄)² = 125 km²

Questions

1   Cube A has a side of 3 cm. Cube B has a side of 5 cm.

   a   What is the ratio of their lengths?

   b   What is the ratio of their areas?

   c   What is the ratio of their volumes?

2   A map is drawn to a scale of 2 cm represents 5 km. A forest has an area of
    60 km². What is the area of the forest on the map?

Answers

1 a 3 : 5   b 3² : 5² → 9 : 25   c 3³ : 5³ → 27 : 125

2 Length ratio 2 cm : 5 km

   Area ratio (2 cm)² : (5 km)²   →   4 cm² : 25 km²

   Therefore   0·16 cm² : 1 km²

                             9.6 cm² : 60 km²   Answer 9.6 cm²

Pythagoras' theorem and trigonometry

Fairly straightforward. They give you the formulae on the exam paper so that makes it easier.

Pythagoras' theorem

When you know the lengths of two sides of a right-angled triangle you can use Pythagoras' theorem to find the third side.

Pythagoras' theorem: $a^2 + b^2 = c^2$ (where c is the longest side)

Note: The longest side is always opposite the right angle.

Examples

Find x

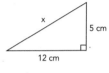

$$5^2 + 12^2 = x^2$$
$$25 + 144 = x^2$$
$$169 = x^2$$
$$\sqrt{169} = x$$
$$13 \text{ cm} = x$$

Find y

$$y^2 + 8^2 = 10^2$$
$$y^2 = 10^2 - 8^2$$
$$y^2 = 100 - 64$$
$$y^2 = 36$$
$$y = \sqrt{36}$$
$$y = 6 \text{ cm}$$

To find the **long** side	To find either **short** side
Square both numbers **Add** them together Take square root of result	Square both numbers **Subtract** the smaller from the larger Take square root of result

Question

1   Find x

2   Find the height of this isosceles triangle:

Answer

1   To find a short side:

Square both numbers 12^2 7^2

Subtract $144 - 49$

(**Note:** Big number – small number.
If you do it the wrong way you will
get "error" when you press $\boxed{\sqrt{}}$)

Square root $\sqrt{95}$

Answer x =   9·75 m

2   An isosceles triangle can be split into
two right–angled triangles.

$$h^2 + 4^2 = 10^2$$
$$h^2 = 10^2 - 4^2$$
$$h^2 = 100 - 16$$
$$h^2 = 84$$
$$h = \sqrt{84}$$
$$h = 9.165 \text{ cm}$$

57

Trigonometry: Finding an angle

This is finding sides and angles. Remember the rules shown. If you are finding an angle you press the TOP LEFT key on your calculator (ie [shift] [INV] or [2nd F] . If you are finding a side you do **not** press the TOP LEFT key on your calculator.

Information similar to this will be given on your examination paper.

Note: This only works for right-angled triangles.

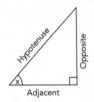

$$SIN = \frac{OPP}{HYP}$$

$$COS = \frac{ADJ}{HYP}$$

$$TAN = \frac{OPP}{ADJ}$$

To find an angle

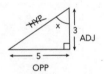

Method

1   Label the triangle
    Hypotenuse = the longest side, opposite the right angle
    Opposite = opposite the angle being used
    Adjacent = next to the angle being used

2   Cross out the side not being used.
    In this question HYP.

3   Look at the formulae in the box at the top.
    Which uses OPP and ADJ?

4   $TAN = \frac{OPP}{ADJ} = \frac{5}{3}$

5   Calculator keys

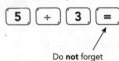 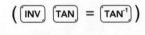

Do **not** forget to press equals

Top left key on most calculators; it will show Shift, Inv or 2nd Function

The answer displayed should be 59.0362... ⟶ 59.0°
If it is not displayed, press [=]

Question

Find x

Answer

$COS = \frac{ADJ}{HYP}$ $\frac{3}{8}$

$= 67.975687...$ ⟶ $68.0°$

Trigonometry: Finding a side

We have used this method before (see page 44).

SIN $= \dfrac{OPP}{HYP}$ → [OPP / SIN X HYP] Cover up what you want and the formula will appear,

eg cover up OPP [SIN X HYP] OPP = SIN x HYP

COS $= \dfrac{ADJ}{HYP}$ → [ADJ / COS X HYP] or cover up HYP

TAN $= \dfrac{OPP}{ADJ}$ → [OPP / TAN X ADJ] [OPP / SIN X] HYP $= \dfrac{OPP}{SIN}$

To find a side

10 m x 28°

HYP 10 m x OPP 28° ADJ

Method

1 Label the triangle
   Hypotenuse = the longest side, opposite the right angle
   Opposite = opposite the angle being used
   Adjacent = next to the angle being used

2 You need the side you are finding (x).
   You need the side you know (10 m).
   Cross out the side not being used. In this question ADJ.

3 Look at the formulae above. Which uses OPP and HYP?

4 We need OPP, cover up OPP to find the formula:

[SIN X HYP] OPP = SIN x HYP
             OPP = SIN28° x 10

5 Calculator keys

[2] [8] [SIN] [x] [1] [0] [=]

This should give you an answer 4·6947.. ⟶ 4·69 m

Note: If this does not work ask your teacher to show you how to work your calculator.

Question

x 40° 8 m

Find x

Answer

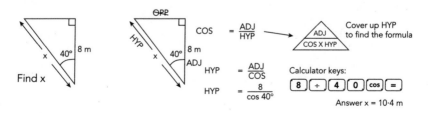

OPP
HYP x 40° 8 m ADJ

COS $= \dfrac{ADJ}{HYP}$ → [ADJ / COS X HYP] Cover up HYP to find the formula

HYP $= \dfrac{ADJ}{COS}$

HYP $= \dfrac{8}{\cos 40°}$

Calculator keys:

[8] [÷] [4] [0] [cos] [=]

Answer x = 10·4 m

Trigonometry: Solving problems

Some questions will involve bearings. These are explained on page 37.

This diagram shows a man at the top of a cliff looking down at a boat.

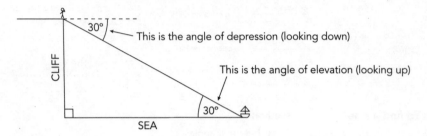

This is the angle of depression (looking down)

This is the angle of elevation (looking up)

Note: The angle of depression from the top of the cliff is equal to the angle of elevation from the boat. (Remember Z angles from page 36.)

Angles of depression and angles of elevation are measured from the horizontal.

Answering questions

1   Read the question carefully.

2   It may help to visualise what is required. You can use objects such as pencils, rubbers, rulers to make a model of what is required.

3   Draw a diagram. Remember you need a right-angled triangle.

4   Read the question again. Check that your diagram is correct.

Question

Sarah is flying a kite. The string is 80 m long and the angle of elevation is 32°. How high is the kite?

Answer

Draw a diagram.

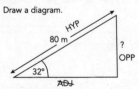

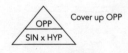

Cover up OPP

OPP = SIN x HYP
= SIN32° x 80
= 42·4 m

Trigonometry and Pythagoras' theorem for 3-D shapes

When you are working with 3-D shapes it helps to visualise the question. If it is a cuboid, your classroom is probably a cuboid so you can visualise the situation. It may help to imagine the shape on your desk, using pencils for flagsticks, or the edge of your desk to the floor for a cliff with a ship at sea, etc. Make sure you understand the question before you start. The best way to explain is to do some questions.

Questions

This diagram shows a horizontal rectangular playground ABCD. At one corner there is a vertical flagstick.

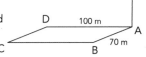

1   The angle of elevation of the top of the flagstick F from the ground at D is 18°. Find the height of the flagstick.

2   A bird is sitting on the ground at C. Calculate:

  a   the angle of elevation from the bird to the top of the flagstick F

  b   the distance the bird must fly (in a straight line) to reach the top of the flagstick F.

Answers

The question states "rectangular playground ABCD" this means the angles are all right angles, even though they don't look 90°. Build a model. Use your desk for the playground, place a ruler or pencil in the far right corner, that is the flagstick. It is much easier to do 3-D questions if we have a 3-D model.

1   This is ordinary trigonometry. Draw a diagram to help

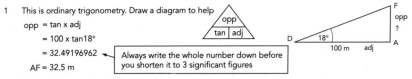

opp = tan x adj

  = 100 x tan18°

  = 32.49196962

AF = 32.5 m

Always write the whole number down before you shorten it to 3 significant figures

Remember to put the whole answer into your calculator memory.
You may need to use it again (do not work with the shortened answer 32·5).

2   a   Look at your model (desk and ruler). Find the right-angled triangle you need. First you need to calculate AC.

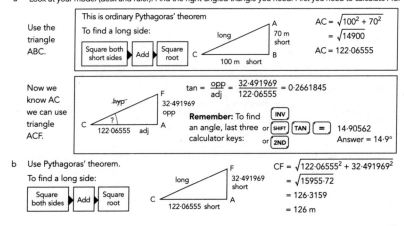

Sine, cosine and tangent of any angle – 1

You must memorise these graphs.
In an emergency you can draw them by using your calculator, eg for sin find values at 45° intervals, ie 0°, 45°, 90°... , 360°

> You can remember these important facts by looking at the graphs.

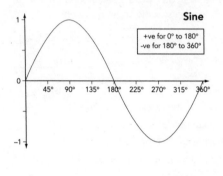

Sine

> +ve for 0° to 180°
> -ve for 180° to 360°

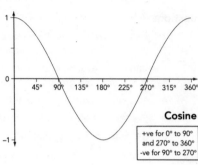

Cosine

> +ve for 0° to 90°
> and 270° to 360°
> -ve for 90° to 270°

Tangent

> +ve for 0° to 90°
> and 180° to 270°
> -ve for 90° to 180°
> and 270° to 360°

Look at the symmetry of all three graphs.

The graphs continue the same symmetrical patterns for negative angles and angles greater than 360°.

Notice there are no values for tangents at 90°, 270°, 450°, etc.

You can use the graphs to find angles.

Suppose you are given the question sin x = 0·4. Find values of x between 0° and 360°.

Method: Draw a horizontal line at 0·4. This gives approximate values x = 25° and x = 155°

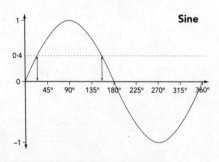

Sine

> **Note:** You would use the same method if you were given the graph of
> y = 2cosx and asked "2cosx = 0·4. Find the value of x".

Note: By extending the graphs above you can find values above 360° and negative values.

Sine, cosine and tangent of any angle – 2

Questions

1   Cos 20° = 0·9396926. Find the angles between 0° and 360° where
cos x° = −0·9396926

2   Tan 130° = −1.1917535. Find four angles where tan x° = 1·1917535

3   Sin x° = −0·4694715. Find two values of x between 0° and 360°

4   Draw the graph of y = 2cos x − 1 for 0 ≤ x ≤360 using 30° intervals and hence find
values of x for which 2cos x − 1 = −1·5

Answers

1   If you have one value for an angle, eg cos 20° = 0.9396926. You can find the "friends" of 20° like this.

Between	Method	Angle
0° - 90°	20°	20°
90° - 180°	180° − 20°	160°
180° - 270°	180° + 20°	200°
270° - 360°	360° − 20°	340°

The cos of all of these angles will be 0.9396926
but two will be +ve and two will be −ve

Either use the cosine graph you have memorised or check using your calculator,

cos 20°   0.9396926 (+ve)
cos 160°   −0.9396926 (−ve)
cos 200°   −0.9396926 (−ve)
cos 340°   0.9396926 (+ve)

Answer 160° and 200°

It is always	0° - 90°	angle
	90° - 180°	180 − angle
	180° - 270°	180 + angle
	270° - 360°	360 − angle

2   You are given "friend 2" (90° - 180°). Friend 2 is 180° − ? = 130°. So "friend 1" = 50°

Between	Method	Angle	
0° - 90°	must be	= 50°	1.1917535
90° - 180°	given as	= 130°	−1.1917535
180° - 270°	180° + 50°	= 230°	1.1917535
270° - 360°	360° − 50°	= 310°	−1.1917535

Use the tangent graph you have
memorised or your calculator to find
which are +ve and which are −ve.

Answer is 50° and 230°. To find other values, keep adding or subtracting 360°,
eg 50° − 360° = −310°, 230° + 360° = 590°.

3   Put −0.469471562 into your calculator then press This will give −28°. (If the calculator
gives a −ve value, the 0° - 90° value
will be the same angle but
positive, ie 28°.)

Between	Method	Angle	
0° - 90°		= 28°	0.4694715
90° - 180°	180° − 28°	= 152°	0.4694715
180° - 270°	180° + 28°	= 208°	−0.4694715
270° - 360°	360° − 28°	= 332°	−0.4694715

Use the sine graph you have
memorised or your calculator
to find which are −ve.

Answer = x = 208° or 332°

Sine, cosine and tangent of any angle – 3

Answers (continued)

4   You need a table of values. If you need a very accurate graph you should use 10° intervals.

If not, intervals of 30° will be satisfactory. The question will normally indicate the level of accuracy.

x	0°	30°	60°	90°	120°	150°	180°	210°	240°	270°	300°	330°	360°
y = 2cosx − 1	1	0·73	0	−1	−2	−2·73	−3	−2·73	−2	−1	0	0·73	1

Example: calculator keys for 150°: [2] [x] [1] [5] [0] [cos] [−] [1] [=]   Answer: −2·73

Draw the graph

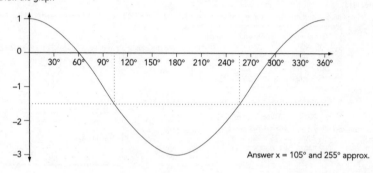

Answer x = 105° and 255° approx.

Sine rule, cosine rule, area of a triangle – 1

Important: If the triangle has a right-angle use ordinary trigonometry (see pages 58-60). If the triangle does not have a right-angle use sine or cosine rule.

Remember if you are given two angles you can easily find the third because angles in a triangle add up to 180°. (This is obvious but many candidates forget this in the exam.)

80°
35°

Remember to label your triangle ABC when you use the sine or cosine rule. It does not matter where you put A, B and C **but**, side a must be opposite angle A, side b must be opposite angle B, and side c must be opposite angle C.

C
a
b
B
c
A

These formulae will be given on the exam paper.

Sine rule

$$\frac{a}{\sin A} = \frac{b}{\sin B} = \frac{c}{\sin C}$$

Use any pair eg $\dfrac{b}{\sin B} = \dfrac{c}{\sin C}$

Cosine rule

$$\cos A = \frac{b^2 + c^2 - a^2}{2bc}$$ ← Use this to find a side

$$a^2 = b^2 + c^2 - 2bc \cos A$$ ← Use this to find an angle

Advice: if you are finding an angle it helps to write the formula upside down:

$$\frac{\sin B}{b} = \frac{\sin C}{c}$$

Use cosine rule

To find a side:
You need two sides and the angle opposite the side you are trying to find

To find an angle:
You need three sides.

Use sine rule

To find a side:
You need one side and two angles

To find an angle:
You need one angle and two sides, ie two sides and two angles including the one you are finding.

You will be given this formula:
Area of a triangle = ¹/₂ ab sin C

Example   Area = ¹/₂ ab sin C
                        = ¹/₂ x a x b x sin C
7 cm 130° 5 cm   = ¹/₂ x 7 x 5 x sin 130°
                        = 13·4 cm²

Questions Find x

1
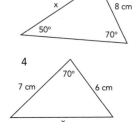

2
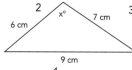

3
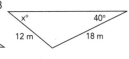

4

5

6 Find the area of this triangle
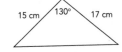

Sine rule, cosine rule, area of a triangle – 2

Answers

1   We are finding a side. We know one side
    and two angles. This suggests **sine rule**.
    Get into the habit of always labelling what
    we are finding, ie side a or angle A.

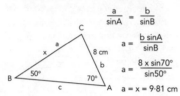

$$\frac{a}{sinA} = \frac{b}{sinB}$$

$$a = \frac{b\ sinA}{sinB}$$

$$a = \frac{8 \times sin70°}{sin50°}$$

$$a = x = 9·81\ cm$$

2   We are finding an angle. We know three sides. This
    suggests **cosine rule**. Label the triangle.

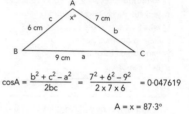

$$cosA = \frac{b^2 + c^2 - a^2}{2bc} = \frac{7^2 + 6^2 - 9^2}{2 \times 7 \times 6} = 0·047619$$

$$A = x = 87·3°$$

3   We are finding an angle. We know two sides
    and one angle. This suggests **sine rule**.
    Label the triangle.

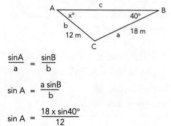

$$\frac{sinA}{a} = \frac{sinB}{b}$$

$$sin\ A = \frac{a\ sinB}{b}$$

$$sin\ A = \frac{18 \times sin40°}{12}$$

$$A = x = 74·6°$$

4   We are finding a side. We know two sides and the
    angle opposite the side we are finding. This
    suggests **cosine rule**. Label the triangle.

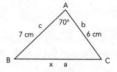

$$a^2 = b^2 + c^2 - 2bc\ cosA$$

$$a^2 = 6^2 + 7^2 - 2 \times 6 \times 7\ cos70°$$

$$a^2 = 56·3$$

$$a = \sqrt{56·3} \qquad a = x = 7·50\ cm$$

5   At first glance we have insufficient
    information. But, remember if we know
    two angles we can easily find the third
    angle. The missing angle is 50°.

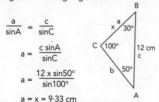

$$\frac{a}{sinA} = \frac{c}{sinC}$$

$$a = \frac{c\ sinA}{sinC}$$

$$a = \frac{12 \times sin50°}{sin100°}$$

$$a = x = 9·33\ cm$$

6   Label the triangle.

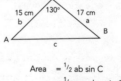

$$\begin{aligned}
Area &= ½\ ab\ sin\ C \\
&= ½ \times a \times b \times sin\ C \\
&= ½ \times 17 \times 15 \times sin\ 130° \\
&= 97·7\ cm^2
\end{aligned}$$

Vectors

A vector is a quantity which has size and direction (ie a length in a direction).

Vectors – 1

A vector can be written $\begin{pmatrix} 2 \\ 3 \end{pmatrix}$ *or* $\underset{\sim}{a}$ *or* $\overrightarrow{AB}$

Let vector $\underset{\sim}{a} = \begin{pmatrix} 2 \\ 3 \end{pmatrix}$ This means 2 along and 3 up. The two vectors shown are both equal to vector $\underset{\sim}{a}$

If vector $\underset{\sim}{c} = \begin{pmatrix} 3 \\ -5 \end{pmatrix}$ vector $4\underset{\sim}{c} = \begin{pmatrix} 12 \\ -20 \end{pmatrix}$ and vector $-\underset{\sim}{c} = \begin{pmatrix} -3 \\ 5 \end{pmatrix}$

vector $\underset{\sim}{a}$ + vector $\underset{\sim}{c} =$ $\begin{pmatrix} 2 \\ 3 \end{pmatrix}$ + $\begin{pmatrix} 3 \\ -5 \end{pmatrix}$ → | add top line <br> add bottom line | → $\begin{pmatrix} 5 \\ -2 \end{pmatrix}$

Speed is distance travelled in a given time. It is not a vector.
Velocity is distance in a specified direction travelled in a given time. It is a vector.

Although technically incorrect you can assume **speed** and **velocity** mean the **same thing** in a GCSE Maths question.

If you have a question with forces or speed or velocity you must draw a triangle.

| These are the forces or speeds or velocities that produce the actual or resultant force or velocity.

 Note: We add them together (arrows in the same direction) to produce the actual or resultant force or speed or velocity. | | This is the resultant force or speed and the direction, ie what actually happens. If it is a plane or ship this is the actual direction and speed or velocity. |

Remember: If we are trying to find the result, arrows go in the same direction.

If we know the actual or resultant force or velocity and another force or velocity, we join the arrows tip to tip.

Example 1   A plane is heading   The wind is blowing
south at 200 km/h   east at 50 km/h

What is the actual direction and speed of the plane?

We are finding the actual direction and speed. Vectors go in the same direction. It will give the same answer if we do this:

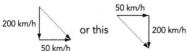 or this

| **Note:** The arrows point in the same direction. These would be wrong. | |

We now use *Pythagoras' theorem and trigonometry* (pages 57–60) and *Bearings* (page 37).

Vectors – 2

Example 2

A plane flies from Acton Airport to Bourne Airport. Bourne Airport is 600 km due south of Acton Airport. The journey takes three hours. There is a wind blowing east at 50 km/h. Find the direction in which the plane must fly and the airspeed (ie speed in still air).

Method: 600 km in 3 hours is an actual speed of 200 km/h. We have an actual speed so vectors are joined tip to tip.

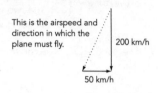

This is the airspeed and direction in which the plane must fly.

200 km/h

50 km/h

We now use Pythagoras' theorem and trigonometry.
Answer: Direction 194°, airspeed 206 km/h.

Example 3

It works exactly the same if we have forces.
Two forces are pulling the object,
calculate the resultant force and direction.

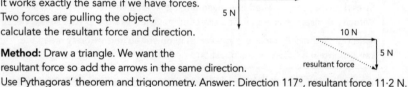

10 N

5 N

10 N

5 N

resultant force

Method: Draw a triangle. We want the resultant force so add the arrows in the same direction.
Use Pythagoras' theorem and trigonometry. Answer: Direction 117°, resultant force 11·2 N.

Note: If velocities or forces are not at right angles proceed in the same way. But you will have to use sine rules or cosine rules instead of Pythagoras' theorem and trigonometry (see sine rules, cosine rules, pages 65 and 66).

Questions

Write the following vectors in the form $\begin{pmatrix} x \\ y \end{pmatrix}$

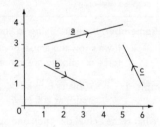

1 a $\underset{\sim}{a}$ b $\underset{\sim}{b}$ c $\underset{\sim}{c}$

   d $3\underset{\sim}{c}$ e $\underset{\sim}{a} - \underset{\sim}{c}$ f $3\underset{\sim}{a} + 2\underset{\sim}{b}$

2 $\overrightarrow{AB} = \underset{\sim}{a}$ $\overrightarrow{BC} = \underset{\sim}{b}$

   D is the midpoint of AB
   E is the midpoint of BC
   F is the midpoint of AC

   a Write the following in terms of $\underset{\sim}{a}$ and $\underset{\sim}{b}$

      i $\overrightarrow{AC}$ ii $\overrightarrow{BD}$ iii $\overrightarrow{BE}$

      iv $\overrightarrow{DC}$ v $\overrightarrow{DE}$

   b Prove that $\overrightarrow{DE}$ is parallel to $\overrightarrow{AC}$

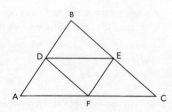

Vectors – 3

Questions (continued)

3   A ship can sail at 30 km/h in still water. The ship heads due north.
    The water current is flowing at 10 km/h due east.

    a   What is the actual velocity of the ship?
    b   What direction does the ship sail in?

4   A boat needs to sail due north from A to B.
    The current is flowing due east at 4 m/s.
    The boat sails at 10 m/s.

    a   What direction must the boat head?
    b   How long does the journey take?

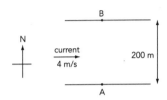

Answers

1   a $\begin{pmatrix} 4 \\ 1 \end{pmatrix}$ b $\begin{pmatrix} 2 \\ -1 \end{pmatrix}$ c $\begin{pmatrix} -1 \\ 2 \end{pmatrix}$ d $3 \times \begin{pmatrix} -1 \\ 2 \end{pmatrix} = \begin{pmatrix} -3 \\ 6 \end{pmatrix}$

     e $\begin{pmatrix} 4 \\ 1 \end{pmatrix} - \begin{pmatrix} -1 \\ 2 \end{pmatrix} = \begin{pmatrix} 5 \\ -1 \end{pmatrix}$ f $3 \times \begin{pmatrix} 4 \\ 1 \end{pmatrix} + 2 \times \begin{pmatrix} 2 \\ -1 \end{pmatrix} = \begin{pmatrix} 12 \\ 3 \end{pmatrix} + \begin{pmatrix} 4 \\ -2 \end{pmatrix} = \begin{pmatrix} 16 \\ 1 \end{pmatrix}$

2   **Remember:** All you have to do is use known routes

     a   i   We know $\overrightarrow{AB}$ and $\overrightarrow{BC}$. Find a way from A to C
               along **known** routes: A to B then B to C

               $\overrightarrow{AC} = \overrightarrow{AB} + \overrightarrow{BC}$

               $\overrightarrow{AC} = \underline{a} + \underline{b}$

> **Note:** When you find an answer,
> ie $\overrightarrow{BE} = \frac{1}{2} \underline{b}$ in part iii, this becomes
> a known route. This is used in part iv.

       ii $\overrightarrow{AB} = \underline{a}$ iii   BE is half of BC

            therefore $\overrightarrow{BA} = -\underline{a}$ (opposite direction) $\overrightarrow{BC} = \underline{b}$

            B to D is half of B to A   therefore $\overrightarrow{BE} = \frac{1}{2} \underline{b}$

            therefore $\overrightarrow{BD} = -\frac{1}{2} \underline{a}$

       iv   Find a way from D to C along   v   Find a way from D to E along
            known routes: D to B then B to C   known routes: D to B then B to E

            $\overrightarrow{DC} = \overrightarrow{DB} + \overrightarrow{BC}$ $\overrightarrow{DE} = \overrightarrow{DB} + \overrightarrow{BE}$

            $\overrightarrow{DC} = \frac{1}{2}\underline{a} + \underline{b}$ $\overrightarrow{DE} = \frac{1}{2}\underline{a} + \frac{1}{2}\underline{b}$

     b $\overrightarrow{AC} = \underline{a} + \underline{b}$ $\overrightarrow{DE} = \frac{1}{2}\underline{a} + \frac{1}{2}\underline{b}$

            $2\overrightarrow{DE} = 2(\frac{1}{2}\underline{a} + \frac{1}{2}\underline{b}) = \underline{a} + \underline{b}$ Therefore DE is parallel to AC

Vectors – 4

Answers (continued)

3 | **Very important:** We are finding the actual velocity. Arrows go in the same direction. | This is a common error. These are wrong:

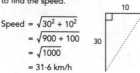

Draw the vector for the ship.
Then add the vector for the current.

Now complete the triangle.

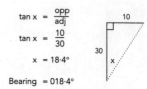

| If you do not have right angles, you will have to use the sine rule or cosine rule (see pages 65 and 66). |

a Use Pythagoras' theorem to find the speed.

$$\text{Speed} = \sqrt{30^2 + 10^2}$$
$$= \sqrt{900 + 100}$$
$$= \sqrt{1000}$$
$$= 31 \cdot 6 \text{ km/h}$$

b

$$\tan x = \frac{\text{opp}}{\text{adj}}$$
$$\tan x = \frac{10}{30}$$
$$x = 18 \cdot 4°$$

Bearing $= 018 \cdot 4°$

4 Think carefully. You need a diagram.

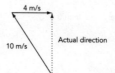

| **Note:** You are finding the actual velocity so arrows go in the same direction. |

| Boat must head in this direction (its actual direction will be north). |

a Use trigonometry

$$\sin x = \frac{\text{opp}}{\text{hyp}}$$
$$\sin x = \frac{4}{10}$$
$$x = 23 \cdot 6°$$

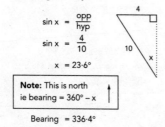

| **Note:** This is north ie bearing $= 360° - x$ |

Bearing $= 336 \cdot 4°$

b First use Pythagoras' theorem to find how far the boat travels in one second

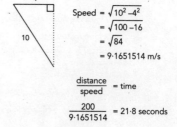

$$\text{Speed} = \sqrt{10^2 - 4^2}$$
$$= \sqrt{100 - 16}$$
$$= \sqrt{84}$$
$$= 9 \cdot 1651514 \text{ m/s}$$

$$\frac{\text{distance}}{\text{speed}} = \text{time}$$

$$\frac{200}{9 \cdot 1651514} = 21 \cdot 8 \text{ seconds}$$

Locus

A couple of ruler and pair of compasses constructions. That's it. Very easy once you know how.

Locus (plural loci)

This is a mathematical name to describe the set of points which satisfy conditions. You will need to use a pair of compasses. Do NOT rub out your construction lines.

Questions

1   Draw the locus of a point which is always 0·75 cm from the line AB.

  A ——————————————— B

2   Draw the locus of a point which is always an equal distance from two points P and Q which are 4 cm apart.

3   Draw the locus of a point which is always an equal distance from the lines BA and BC.

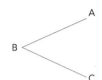

Answers

1   You must use a pair of compasses to draw the semi-circles at each end.

2

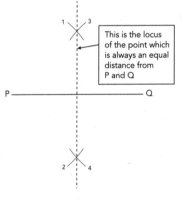

This is the locus of the point which is always an equal distance from P and Q

3

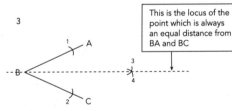

This is the locus of the point which is always an equal distance from BA and BC

Method

a   Open a pair of compasses. Keep them the same distance apart.
b   Place the pair of compasses on B.
c   Draw an arc on AB (1).
d   Draw an arc on BC (2).
e   Place the pair of compasses at 1 where the arc crosses the line AB.
f   Draw an arc (3).
g   Place the pair of compasses at 2 where the arc crosses the line BC.
h   Draw an arc (4).
i   Join B to the intersection of arcs 3 and 4.

Method

a   Join P and Q.
b   Place a pair of compasses on P.
c   Open the compasses over halfway towards Q.
d   Draw an arc above and below the line (1 and 2).
e   Keep the compasses the same distance apart.
f   Place the pair of compasses on Q.
g   Draw an arc above and below the line (3 and 4).
h   Join the intersections of both arcs. This is the locus.

Advice: Make sure you have a tight pair of compasses – drawing an arc is impossible if your compass slips.

Questionnaires

This may be useful for your coursework. It is quite easy. Just use your common sense.

Designing questionnaires

Questionnaires are used to obtain information. You may need to design a questionnaire as part of your coursework.

1   Design your questions to obtain information you can present and analyse in a variety of ways. A variety of different ways to present your data is given on pages 75-79 and 82.

2   Make your questions easy to understand.

3   Do not ask embarrassing questions, eg "How many boyfriends do you have?"

4   Provide a choice of answer, eg "Do you do a lot of homework?", will produce answers such as "yes", "sometimes", "only in Maths". These responses are difficult to present and analyse. A better question would be:

   "How much time did you spend doing homework last night? Tick the box nearest to the amount of time."

   0 hours ☐   1 hours ☐   2 hours ☐   3 hours ☐

Types of question

Your questionnaire should contain one or two questions of each of the following types:

1   Questions with yes/no responses, eg "Do you own a bicycle?" Yes ☐ No ☐

   Try to avoid questions to which everyone will answer yes or everyone will answer no. Your results can be shown as a percentage, in a bar graph, pictogram, pie chart, etc.

2   Questions with numerical answers, eg "How many televisions do you have in your house?"

   Your results can be presented in graphs, tables, etc. You can calculate the mean, median and mode of the data.

3   Questions you can compare, eg "What was your percentage mark in the English exam?" and "What was your percentage mark in the Maths exam?"

   These questions will allow you to draw a scatter diagram to test a hypothesis such as "Pupils who obtain high marks in English also obtain high marks in Maths."

How many people to ask

Twenty is a good number. Each person represents 5% of the total and each person can be represented by 18° on a pie chart.

Forty is a good number. Each person represents 2·5% of the total and each person can be represented by 9° on a pie chart.

How many questions to ask

A maximum of ten.

Sampling

Census: Data is collected from everything.

Random sampling: Data is chosen at random.

Systematic: Select a sample, eg every tenth person in a queue, every
                        hundredth person on a list.

Stratified random sampling

Example

A sixth form has 200 students:

- 60 study A-Levels
- 90 study GNVQ
- 50 study BTEC

A survey of 20 students is taken.

Use stratified random sampling to decide how many students from each course
should be sampled.

Method

We are sampling 20 out of 200. Therefore multiply. by $^{20}/_{200}$.

$60 \times {}^{20}/_{200} = 6$ A-Level students should be randomly selected

$90 \times {}^{20}/_{200} = 9$ GNVQ students should be randomly selected

$50 \times {}^{20}/_{200} = 5$ BTEC students should be randomly selected

Question

500 people watch a film:

160 are men, 120 are women, 180 are boys, 40 are girls.

A survey of 25 people is taken. Use stratified random sampling to decide how many
men, women, boys and girls should be surveyed.

Answer

Men	$160 \times {}^{25}/_{500} = 8$
Women	$120 \times {}^{25}/_{500} = 6$
Boys	$180 \times {}^{25}/_{500} = 9$
Girls	$40 \times {}^{25}/_{500} = 2$

Hypotheses

A hypothesis is an idea. Hypotheses can be tested in a variety of ways, eg observation, experiment, questionnaire.

Task

Choose a hypothesis. Decide how to test it. Collect data. Present the data in a variety of ways (see pages 75-79 and 82). Analyse the data. Draw conclusions. Was the hypothesis correct?

What to do

1   Think of a hypothesis. A hypothesis is a statement or observation which may be true, eg "More men than women drive cars", "A drawing-pin lands point upwards more than point downwards", "Girls' favourite television channel is BBC1".

2   Decide how to test your hypothesis. How will you collect your data?
    The above hypotheses could be tested in these ways:

    • More men than women drive cars (observation).
    • A drawing-pin lands point upwards more than point downwards (experiment).
    • Girls' favourite television channel is BBC1 (questionnaire).

3   How will you analyse and present your data? The following should be included:

    • Tables – eg percentages
    • Graphs – pictograms, bar charts, line graphs
    • Pie charts – including your calculations
    • Frequency polygons
    • Averages – mean, median, mode
    • Range
    • Scatter diagrams – positive correlation, negative correlation, line of best fit
    • Cumulative frequency – upper quartile, lower quartile, inter-quartile range
    • Bias – are the results honest? For example, a coin could be weighted to give more heads than tails. If a teacher conducts a survey "How many hours of homework did you do last night?", some pupils might lie.

    If you can use a computer you could include spreadsheets, etc.

    Remember to make your graphs neat; try to use colour.

    Do not produce dozens of one type of graph. It is far better to draw three or four pie charts than 20 pie charts.

    Remember to state your hypothesis at the start.

    Remember to analyse your findings. Draw conclusions from your results. Justify your conclusions – is your hypothesis proved?

If your hypothesis does not allow you to analyse and present your data in a variety of ways it is far wiser to choose a different hypothesis **immediately**. Do not waste time on a hypothesis which will not allow you to demonstrate your mathematical ability.

Tables and graphs

Again much of this is common sense. You need to be able to read information from tables and graphs in everyday life.

Comparing data

Sometimes you will be asked to compare two sets of data. If you are comparing you must write about the similarities and differences of BOTH sets of data. A frequency polygon is a graph produced by joining up points with straight lines.

Questions

The heights of 20 boys and 20 girls aged 16 are shown in this table:

Height (cm)	Number of boys	Number of girls
140 – 149	–	1
150 – 159	1	3
160 – 169	6	8
170 – 179	8	6
180 – 189	4	2
190 – 199	1	–

1 Present the data in a frequency polygon.

2 Compare the distributions and comment on your findings.

Answers

1

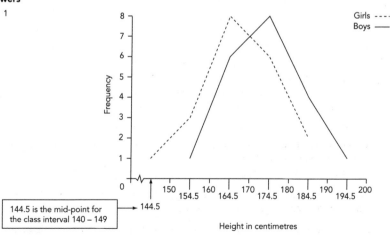

144.5 is the mid-point for the class interval 140 – 149 → 144.5

Height in centimetres

2 The frequency polygon shows that boys aged 16 are generally taller than girls of the same age.

Histograms

> **Note:** In a **bar graph** the frequency is the **height** of each bar.
> In a **histogram** the frequency is the **area** of each bar.

Questions

1 This table shows the ages of people in a room.
Draw a histogram to show this information.

Age	Frequency
$0 \leq x < 10$	4
$10 \leq x < 30$	6
$30 \leq x < 60$	6
$60 \leq x < 80$	8

2 This histogram shows the height of people in a room:

a How many people were
between 140 cm and 150 cm?
b How many people were
between 150 cm and 180 cm?
c How many people were
between 180 cm and 200 cm?
d How many people were in the room?

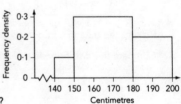

Answers

1 First calculate the frequency density (frequency density = frequency ÷ age range)

Age	Frequency	Frequency density
$0 \leq x < 10$	4	$4 \div 10 = 0{\cdot}4$
$10 \leq x < 30$	6	$6 \div 20 = 0{\cdot}3$
$30 \leq x < 60$	6	$6 \div 30 = 0{\cdot}2$
$60 \leq x < 80$	8	$8 \div 20 = 0{\cdot}4$

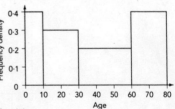

2 We find the number of people by calculating the area of each bar.

a Area is 10 x 0.1 = 1 person
b Area is 30 x 0.3 = 9 people
c Area is 20 x 0.2 = 4 people
d 1 + 9 + 4 = 14 people

Grouped data

Information is often grouped. We can estimate the median, mean and range.

Questions

This table shows the number of cars using a car park over a period of 100 days:

Number of cars	0 – 99	100 – 199	200 – 299	300 – 399	400 – 500
Frequency	5	18	30	27	20

1   What is the modal class?
2   Estimate the median.
3   Estimate the mean.

Answers

1   The modal class is the class with the highest number. In this question it is 200 – 299 cars.
2   There are 100 days. The median is the middle day when arranged in order of size. The question asks for an estimate, therefore we can assume that the median is the 50th day.
    5 + 18 = 23. Therefore there are 23 days with less than 200 cars.
    5 + 18 + 30 = 53. Therefore there are 53 days with less than 300 cars.
    The 50th day is towards the high end of the 200 – 299 class.
    A good estimate of the median would be about 290 cars.
3   The mean is found by first multiplying the mid-value of each class by the frequency. The question asks for an estimate, therefore we can use 50, 150, 250, 350 and 450 as the mid–values.

$$\frac{(5 \times 50) + (18 \times 150) + (30 \times 250) + (27 \times 350) + (20 \times 450)}{100}$$

$$= \frac{250 + 2700 + 7500 + 9450 + 9000}{100}$$

$$= \frac{28900}{100}$$

The mean number of cars is about 289.

Cumulative frequency

Cumulative frequency is very likely to appear on your exam paper. Just learn the rules.

Cumulative frequency

We can use cumulative frequency curves to compare data.

Questions

This table shows the marks of pupils in an exam:

Mark	Frequency
6-15	3
16-25	10
26-35	14
36-45	28
46-55	20
56-65	5

1 What is the range of the marks?

2 Draw a cumulative frequency diagram.

3 What is the median mark?

4 What is the upper quartile?

5 What is the lower quartile?

6 What is the interquartile range?

7 Pupils need 50 or over for an 'A' grade. How many 'A' grades were awarded?

Answers

1 The range is 65 – 6 = 59

2 First complete a cumulative frequency column

Mark	Frequency	Cumulative Frequency
6-15	3	3
16-25	10	3+10 = 13
26-35	14	3+10+14 = 27
36-45	28	3+10+14+28 = 55
46-55	20	3+10+14+28+20 = 75
56-65	5	3+10+14+28+20+5 = 80

Note: Points are plotted at the maximum value of the class interval, eg the 46–55 interval is plotted at (55,75) not (50,75).

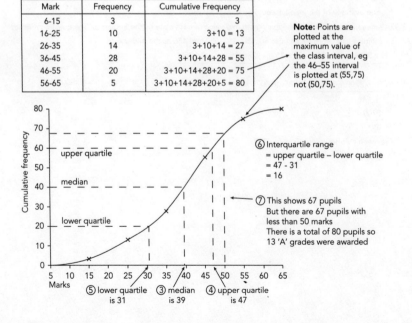

⑥ Interquartile range
= upper quartile – lower quartile
= 47 - 31
= 16

⑦ This shows 67 pupils
But there are 67 pupils with less than 50 marks
There is a total of 80 pupils so 13 'A' grades were awarded

⑤ lower quartile is 31

③ median is 39

④ upper quartile is 47

Using cumulative frequency diagrams to compare distributions

Question

Two different makes of light bulbs were compared. The cumulative frequency diagrams show the number of hours the bulbs lasted.

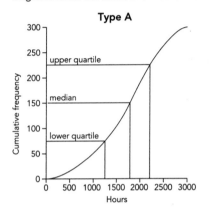

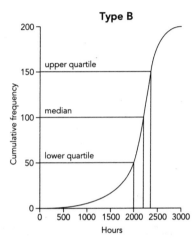

Use the median and interquartile range to compare the two distributions.

Answer

Different numbers of bulbs were used in the tests but the median and interquartile range allow comparison between the two types of bulb. The interquartile range measures the range of the middle half of the distribution.

The median of bulb A is about 1800 hours.
The median of bulb B is about 2200 hours.
This implies that bulb B is better because the median bulb lasts 400 hours longer.

The interquartile range of bulb A is about (2200 – 1250) 950 hours.
The interquartile range of bulb B is about (2400 – 2000) 400 hours.

The middle half of bulb B is bunched together, ie steeper curve.
The middle half of bulb A is more spread out.

The information suggests that bulbs of type B are more consistent and have a longer lifetime.

Standard deviation

If your teacher has shown you how to use your calculator to find standard deviation you are advised to ignore this page. A formula will be given on your exam paper. I am going to show you how to use this one: Standard deviation (SD) = $\sqrt{\dfrac{\Sigma x^2}{n} - \left(\dfrac{\Sigma x}{n}\right)^2}$

Ask your teacher if this formula is given on your exam paper. If not you will have to learn it.

Standard deviation

Example Find the standard deviation of these numbers 12, 5, 7, 10, 6.

1	n	Count how many numbers we have		5
2	Σx	Add the numbers (Σ means add)	$12 + 5 + 7 + 10 + 6 =$	40
3	$\dfrac{\Sigma x}{n}$	Divide by n (all we have done so far is find the mean!)	$\dfrac{40}{5} =$	8
4	$\left(\dfrac{\Sigma x}{n}\right)^2$	Square the mean	$8^2 =$	64
5		Put 64 into your calculator memory		
6	Σx^2	Add the numbers squared	$12^2 + 5^2 + 7^2 + 10^2 + 6^2 =$	354
7	$\dfrac{\Sigma x^2}{n}$	Divide by n	$\dfrac{354}{5} =$	70·8
8	$\dfrac{\Sigma x^2}{n} - \left(\dfrac{\Sigma x}{n}\right)^2$	Subtract the mean squared (this number is in calculator memory)	$70·8 - 64 =$	6·8
9	$\sqrt{\dfrac{\Sigma x^2}{n} - \left(\dfrac{\Sigma x}{n}\right)^2}$	Square root	$\sqrt{6·8} =$	2·60768

Question Find the standard deviation of these numbers 5, 7, 3, 10, 4, 6, 12, 4.

Answer

1	n	Count how many numbers we have		8
2	Σx	Add the numbers (Σ means add)	$5 + 7 + 3 + 10 + 4 + 6 + 12 + 4 =$	51
3	$\dfrac{\Sigma x}{n}$	Divide by n (all we have done so far is find the mean!)	$\dfrac{51}{8} =$	6·375
4	$\left(\dfrac{\Sigma x}{n}\right)^2$	Square the mean	$6·375^2 =$	40·6406
5		Put 40·6406 into your calculator memory		
6	Σx^2	Add the numbers squared	$5^2 + 7^2 + 3^2 + 10^2 + 4^2 + 6^2 + 12^2 + 4^2 =$	395
7	$\dfrac{\Sigma x^2}{n}$	Divide by n	$\dfrac{395}{8} =$	49·375
8	$\dfrac{\Sigma x^2}{n} - \left(\dfrac{\Sigma x}{n}\right)^2$	Subtract the mean squared (this number is in calculator memory)	$49·375 - 40·6406 =$	8·73437
9	$\sqrt{\dfrac{\Sigma x^2}{n} - \left(\dfrac{\Sigma x}{n}\right)^2}$	Square root	$\sqrt{8·73437} =$	2·955

The normal distribution

This is a distribution which has the majority of values in the centre and very few at each end.

This graph has a
normal distribution.

SD = standard deviation

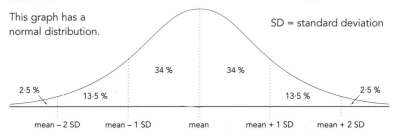

2·5 %			2·5 %
	13·5 %	34 %	34 %	13·5 %	

mean – 2 SD   mean – 1 SD   mean   mean + 1 SD   mean + 2 SD

68% of the data is within 1 standard deviation (1 SD) of the mean.
95% of the data is within 2 standard deviations (2 SD) of the mean.
5% of the data is more than 2 standard deviation (2 SD) from the mean.

Questions

1   Bags of sweets contain a mean of 450 g and are normally distributed with a standard deviation of 4 g.

   a   What are the weights between which the central 68% should lie?

   b   What percentage of bags should contain less than 442 g?

   c   5000 bags of sweets are provided. How many bags are over 458 g?

2   This data shows the heights of two groups of men from different parts of the world:

	Group A	Group B
Mean height	1·72 m	1·75 m
Standard deviation	0·1 m	0·07 m

Comment upon these two sets of data.

Answers

1   a   68% is within 1 SD, ie 4 g either side of the mean, so the central 68% lies between 446 g and 454 g.

   b   442 g is 8 g below the mean, ie 2 standard deviations below the mean. 2·5% of the data is more than 2 standard deviations **below** the mean.

   c   458 g is 8 g above the mean, ie 2 standard deviations above the mean 2·5% of 5000 is 125 bags.

2   **Group A**   **Group B**

   68% have heights between 1·62 m and 1·82 m   68% have heights between 1·68 m and 1·82 m

   95% have heights between 1·52 m and 1·92 m   95% have heights between 1·61 m and 1·89 m

The data shows that Group B has a smaller standard deviation, therefore the data has a tighter distribution, whereas the data in Group A has a higher standard deviation and is more spread out. There are more shorter people in Group A than Group B.

Scatter diagrams

These are used to find connections between two sets of data.

Line of best fit

Scatter diagrams are used to find relationships (or correlation) between two sets of data.

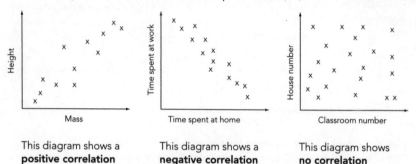

This diagram shows a **positive correlation**

This diagram shows a **negative correlation**

This diagram shows **no correlation**

A line of best fit is drawn by looking at the crosses on a scatter diagram and then drawing a line. Normally there would be a similar number of crosses above the line as below the line.

Questions

1 Draw a line of best fit on this scatter diagram. This scatter diagram shows the masses of 16 pupils against their ages.

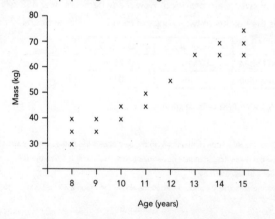

2 Use your line of best fit to estimate the mass of a 13 year old pupil.

Answers

1 The line should be drawn so that there are a similar number of crosses above the line as below the line.

2 **Method:** Draw a line from 13 years to the line of best fit. Read the mass. The answer should be about 60 kg.

Probability

You need to understand when to multiply probabilities, when to add probabilities and tree diagrams.

Estimation of probability by experiment

We can carry out an experiment to help us to estimate probability, eg we could throw a thousand drawing-pins and count how many times they landed point up. This would allow us to use the probability to estimate how many would land point up if a million drawing-pins were thrown.

The more times an experiment is carried out, the more likely the data obtained is accurate.

Example

A six-sided die is thrown. Here are the results:

Side of die	1	2	3	4	5	6
John	2	7	3	8	4	6
Andrea	46	51	53	47	46	57

John threw the die 30 times. Andrea threw the die 300 times.

Andrea is more likely to obtain the better estimate because she has thrown the die more times than John.

Questions

A die is thrown 600 times. These results are obtained.

1	2	3	4	5	6
102	112	181	31	82	92

1 Do the results indicate the die is biased?

2 Justify your answer.

3 Use the data to work out the probability of the die landing on:
a 1, b 3, c 4, d 6

4 If the die were fair how many times would you expect it to land on each number if it were thrown 600 times?

Answers

1 The die seems to be biased.

2 More 3s were obtained than would be expected by chance. Fewer 4s were obtained than would be expected by chance.

3 a $^{102}/_{600} = ^{51}/_{300} = ^{17}/_{100}$ b $^{181}/_{600}$
   c $^{31}/_{600}$ d $^{92}/_{600} = ^{23}/_{150}$

4 We would expect the die to land on each number a similar amount of times. The chance of each number is $^1/_6$. Therefore we would expect each number to occur about 100 times.

Tree diagrams

Tree diagrams can be used to help you work out the probability of events.

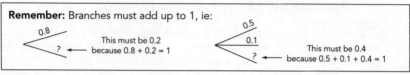

Remember: Branches must add up to 1, ie:

This must be 0.2 because 0.8 + 0.2 = 1

This must be 0.4 because 0.5 + 0.1 + 0.4 = 1

Questions

A car driver passes through two sets of traffic lights on his way to work. The lights can either be red or green. The probability of red at the first lights is 0·6. The probability of red at the second lights is 0·3. Draw a tree diagram to show this and hence calculate the probability that:

1   Both lights are red.

2   Both lights are green.

3   One set of lights is red and one is green.

4   At least one set of lights is red.

Answers

This problem is independent probability. The colour of the second traffic lights is not affected by the colour of the first set.

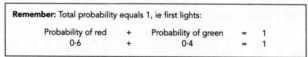

Remember: Total probability equals 1, ie first lights:

| Probability of red | + | Probability of green | = | 1 |
| 0·6 | + | 0·4 | = | 1 |

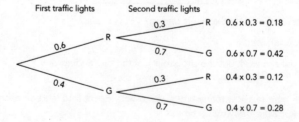

First traffic lights   Second traffic lights

0.6 — R
0.3 — R   0.6 x 0.3 = 0.18
0.7 — G   0.6 x 0.7 = 0.42
0.4 — G
0.3 — R   0.4 x 0.3 = 0.12
0.7 — G   0.4 x 0.7 = 0.28

1   0·18   2   0·28

3   Red and green or green and red   0·42 + 0·12 = 0·54

4   Red and red or red and green or green and red   0·18 + 0·42 + 0·12 = 0·72

Alternative method

The question states "at least". Look at page 87 *Probability (at least)*.

Total probability	–	what we do not want	=	what we do want
1	–	green and green	=	what we do want
1	–	0·28	=	0·72

Conditional and independent probablility

Conditional probability implies that a probability is conditional upon what has happened previously (question 1 below).

Independent probability implies that the probability of one event does not depend upon the outcome of another event (question 2 below).

Questions

1 The probability of a person passing maths is 0·7. The probability of a person who has passed Maths, passing Science is 0·8. The probability of a person who has failed Maths, passing Science is 0·4.

  Draw a tree diagram to show this and hence answer the following questions.

  a What is the probability of a person passing Maths and Science?

  b What is the probability of a person failing Maths and Science?

  c What is the probability of a person passing one subject and failing the other?

2 A man shakes a 6-sided die and tosses a coin. What is the probability that:

  a He shakes a 4 and tosses a tail?

  b He shakes an even number and tosses a tail?

Answers

1

Maths	**Science**		
0·8	pass $\longrightarrow$ (0·7 x 0·8)	$\longrightarrow$ 0·56	
0·7 pass			
0·2	fail $\longrightarrow$ (0·7 x 0·2)	$\longrightarrow$ 0·14	
0·3 fail 0·4	pass $\longrightarrow$ (0·3 x 0·4)	$\longrightarrow$ 0·12	
0·6	fail $\longrightarrow$ (0·3 x 0·6)	$\longrightarrow$ 0·18	

a 0·56

b 0·18

c Pass Maths **and** fail Science **or** fail Maths **and** pass Science.

   0·7   x   0·2   +   0·3   x   0·4   =   0·26

2 a   Probability of shaking a 4   **and**   tossing a tail

   $^1/_6$ x $^1/_2$ = $^1/_{12}$

  b   Probability of shaking an even number   **and**   tossing a tail

   $^1/_2$ x $^1/_2$ = $^1/_4$

85

Probability (and, or)

This method can be used with conditional or independent events.

> **AND** means **MULTIPLY**
> **OR** means **ADD**

Example

A bag contains three red sweets, four blue sweets and five white sweets.

A boy is blindfolded. What is the probability he chooses a blue sweet, eats it, then chooses a red sweet?

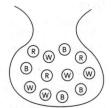

Method

This question is conditional probability. Note how the number of sweets changes when the second sweet is chosen. Try to rephrase the question using the key words:

| BLUE SWEET | RED SWEET | **AND** | **OR** |

The boy needs | BLUE SWEET | **AND** | RED SWEET

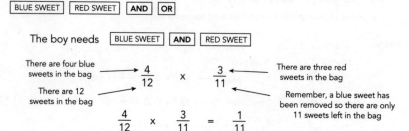

There are four blue sweets in the bag $\longrightarrow \dfrac{4}{12}$ × $\dfrac{3}{11} \longleftarrow$ There are three red sweets in the bag

There are 12 sweets in the bag

Remember, a blue sweet has been removed so there are only 11 sweets left in the bag

$$\dfrac{4}{12} \times \dfrac{3}{11} = \dfrac{1}{11}$$

Questions

1   What is the probability of choosing two red sweets?

2   What is the probability of choosing a red sweet and a white sweet in any order?

Answers

1   Key words | RED SWEET | **AND** | **OR** | Rephrase the question using the key words.

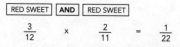

| RED SWEET | **AND** | RED SWEET |

$$\dfrac{3}{12} \times \dfrac{2}{11} = \dfrac{1}{22}$$

2   Key words | RED SWEET | WHITE SWEET | **AND** | **OR** | Rephrase the question using the key words.

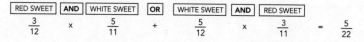

| RED SWEET | **AND** | WHITE SWEET | **OR** | WHITE SWEET | **AND** | RED SWEET |

$$\dfrac{3}{12} \times \dfrac{5}{11} + \dfrac{5}{12} \times \dfrac{3}{11} = \dfrac{5}{22}$$

Probability (at least)

This page shows you a shortcut. This is used when a question asks for the probability of "at least" or the "probability of not getting".

Questions

Three coins are tossed.

What is the probability of:

1   Exactly one head?

2   At least one head?

Answers

1   We need:

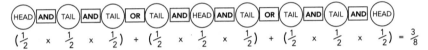

$$(\tfrac{1}{2} \times \tfrac{1}{2} \times \tfrac{1}{2}) + (\tfrac{1}{2} \times \tfrac{1}{2} \times \tfrac{1}{2}) + (\tfrac{1}{2} \times \tfrac{1}{2} \times \tfrac{1}{2}) = \tfrac{3}{8}$$

(Or you could use a tree diagram, see page 84.)

2   Remember, the total probability for all of the possible ways three coins can land is 1. We could say:

HEAD AND HEAD AND HEAD OR HEAD AND HEAD AND TAIL OR . . .

This will work but it takes a long time!

Think carefully

Sometimes it is quicker to work out the probability of what we do not want.

What don't we want?

We don't want three tails. Any other outcome will contain at least one head.

The probability of three tails is:

TAIL AND TAIL AND TAIL

$$\tfrac{1}{2} \times \tfrac{1}{2} \times \tfrac{1}{2} = \tfrac{1}{8}$$

Total probability – Probability of three tails = Probability of at least one head

$$1 \quad - \quad \tfrac{1}{8} \quad = \quad \tfrac{7}{8}$$

> **Note:** When a question states "at least" always consider the short cut
>
> Total probability – what we do not want = what we do want

Supplementary material

This section contains material that is on most Higher Tier exam papers. Ask your teacher if it will be on your exam paper.

3-D co-ordinates

You are used to using 2-D co-ordinates – eg (3, 7) means 3 along the x-axis and 7 along the y-axis. 3-D co-ordinates are the same, but we are locating points in space. The easiest way to understand 3-D co-ordinates such as (3, 7, 2) is to think 3 along the x-axis, 7 along the y-axis and 2 up.

Two dimensional co-ordinates are (x, y)

Three dimensional co-ordinates are (x, y, z)

x and y are normal co-ordinates

z is vertical (ie going up)

Questions

A box is 8 cm long, 6 cm wide and 4 cm high.
The co-ordinate of the bottom left corner is (0, 0, 0)

Give the co-ordinates of:

    1   B   2   C

    3   D   4   The centre of the box

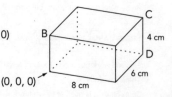

Answers

1   To reach B we go: 0 along the x-axis
                             0 along the y-axis   }   (0, 0, 4)
                             4 along the z-axis

2   To reach C we go: 8 along the x-axis
                             6 along the y-axis   }   (8, 6, 4)
                             4 along the z-axis

3   To reach D we go: 8 along the x-axis
                             6 along the y-axis   }   (8, 6, 0)
                             0 along the z-axis

4   4 along the x-axis
                             3 along the y-axis   }   (4, 3, 2)
                             2 along the z-axis

Inequalities

Equations have a definite solution, inequalities have a range of solutions. Apart from this they are very similar.

> **Note:** The symbol always points to the smaller number

> means greater than
< means less than
≥ means greater than or equal to
≤ means less than or equal to

Always read the question carefully. Sometimes it asks you to shade the wanted region, sometimes the unwanted region. Sometimes it asks you to describe the shaded region, sometimes the unshaded region.

Questions

1 Solve these inequalities:

a $5x > 20$ b $x - 7 < 10$ c $-2x > 8$
d $3 \leq 2x + 1 < 13$ e $x^2 \geq 16$

2 Draw and indicate the following regions by shading:

a $x > 4$ b $y \leq 2$

Answers

1 Inequalities are very similar to equations:

a $\quad 5x > 20$ b $\quad x - 7 < 10$ c $\quad -2x > 8$
$\quad x > {}^{20}/_5$ $\quad x < 10 + 7$ $\quad x < {}^{8}/_{-2}$
$\quad x > 4$ $\quad x < 17$ $\quad x < -4$

Note: When we have a negative multiplication or division the inequality sign reverses. This causes many difficulties. If you are not certain which way the inequality sign should point, try a check. The solution shows x is less than –4. Choose a value less than –4, eg –5:

Is it true that $\qquad -2x > 8$?
ie $\qquad -2 \times -5 > 8$
$\qquad 10 > 8$ Yes, it is true. So $x < -4$ is correct.

d Solve as an equation. $3 \leq \quad 2x + 1 \quad < 13$
Subtract 1 from everything: $3 - 1 \leq 2x + 1 - 1 < 13 - 1$
$\qquad 2 \leq \quad 2x \quad < 12$
Divide everything by 2: $1 \leq \quad x \quad < 6$

e Remember, if $x^2 = 16$ then x can equal 4 or –4, ie $4 \times 4 = 16$, $-4 \times -4 = 16$. Therefore $x \geq 4$, $x \leq -4$

2a

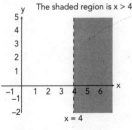

The shaded region is $x > 4$

$x = 4$

Note: We use a dotted line when it is < or >

b

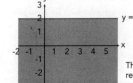

$y = 2$

The shaded region is $y \leq 2$

Note: We use a solid line when it is ≥ or ≤

Critical path analysis

When completing a job, several tasks may need to be carried out. Some tasks may have to be done before others can be started, eg if you were building a shed you would have to lay the foundations before you could erect the shed. You would have to erect the shed before you could build cupboards in the shed. The critical route is the route that takes the longest time.

Questions

This is a network. Each letter represents a job to be completed. The number shows the time, in hours, required to complete each job.

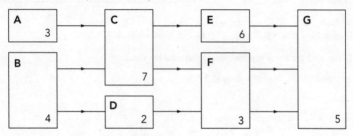

1   What is the critical path?
2   What is the minimum time for the whole job?
3   Draw a priority table for the network.
4   The whole job must be completed by 2300.
    What is the latest possible time job D can start?

Answers

1   Follow each possible route to find the longest:

    A C E G →   21 hours

    A C F G →   18 hours

    B C E G →   22 hours ← this is the longest time, therefore the critical path is BCEG

    B C F G →   19 hours

    B D F G →   14 hours

2   The minimum time is 22 hours

3

Job	These jobs must be done first
A	-
B	-
C	A B
D	B
E	A B C
F	A B C D
G	A B C D E F

4   D + F + G = 2 + 3 + 5 = 10 hours. The latest time job D can start is 1300.

Linear programming

Question

A man must spend a minimum of £1000 on chairs at £20 each and tables at £40 each. He must buy a maximum of 40 items of furniture. At least half of the items of furniture must be chairs.

a   Write three inequalities.

b   Draw a linear programming graph and shade the region which satisfies the inequalities (put tables on the horizontal axis, chairs on the vertical axis).

Answer

C represents chairs, T represents tables

Inequality 1: $40T + 20C \geq 1000$

Plotting this on the graph

Let T = 0 then $C \geq 50$ ⟶   plot the point (0, 50)

Let C = 0 then $T \geq 25$ ⟶   plot the point (25, 0)

Inequality 2: $T + C \leq 40$

Plotting this on the graph

Let T = 0 then $C \leq 40$ ⟶   plot the point (0, 40)

Let C = 0 then $T \leq 40$ ⟶   plot the point (40, 0)

Inequality 3: $T \leq C$

Plotting this on the graph

Let T = 0 then $C \geq 0$ - plot the point (0, 0)

Let C = 0 then $T \leq 0$ - plot the point (0, 0) **Problem:** These are the same points. Choose another value for T:

Let T = 30 then $C \geq 30$ ⟶   plot the point (30, 30)

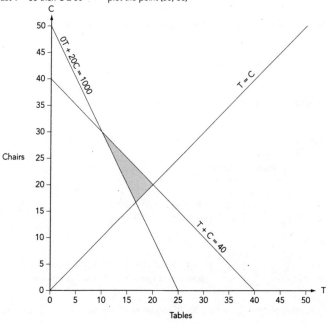

Transformations (matrices) – 1

Rotation matrices

What the matrix does

$\begin{pmatrix} 0 & -1 \\ 1 & 0 \end{pmatrix}$ Rotation 90° anticlockwise (270° clockwise)

$\begin{pmatrix} 0 & 1 \\ -1 & 0 \end{pmatrix}$ Rotation 270° anticlockwise (90° clockwise)

$\begin{pmatrix} -1 & 0 \\ 0 & -1 \end{pmatrix}$ Rotation 180° anticlockwise (180° clockwise)

Enlargement matrices

What the matrix does

$\begin{pmatrix} a & 0 \\ 0 & a \end{pmatrix}$ Enlargement by a scale factor of a

For example:

$\begin{pmatrix} 3 & 0 \\ 0 & 3 \end{pmatrix}$ Enlargement by a scale factor of 3

Reflection matrices

What the matrix does

$\begin{pmatrix} 1 & 0 \\ 0 & -1 \end{pmatrix}$ Reflection in the x-axis

$\begin{pmatrix} -1 & 0 \\ 0 & 1 \end{pmatrix}$ Reflection in the y-axis

$\begin{pmatrix} -1 & 0 \\ 0 & -1 \end{pmatrix}$ Reflection in the x-axis followed by a reflection in the y-axis

$\begin{pmatrix} 0 & 1 \\ 1 & 0 \end{pmatrix}$ Reflection in the line y = x

$\begin{pmatrix} 0 & -1 \\ -1 & 0 \end{pmatrix}$ Reflection in the line y = –x

Multiplying matrices

Memorise this: | Row x Column |

Example $\begin{pmatrix} a & b \\ c & d \end{pmatrix}\begin{pmatrix} e & f \\ g & h \end{pmatrix} = \begin{pmatrix} ae + bg & af + bh \\ ce + dg & cf + dh \end{pmatrix}$

Look how it works:

$\begin{pmatrix} \text{row 1} \\ \text{row 2} \end{pmatrix}\begin{pmatrix} \text{column 1} & \text{column 2} \end{pmatrix} = \begin{pmatrix} \text{row 1 x column 1} & \text{row 1 x column 2} \\ \text{row 2 x column 1} & \text{row 2 x column 2} \end{pmatrix}$

Look: When you multiply row 2 by column 1, you write the answer in row 2, column 1

Transformations (matrices) – 2

Questions

1   The triangle T with coordinates A(5, 1), B(6, 3), C(2, 7) is transformed by the matrix

$$\begin{pmatrix} 0 & -1 \\ -1 & 0 \end{pmatrix}$$ to produce T'

    a   What are the coordinates of T'?

    b   Describe the transformation

2   The triangle R with coordinates A(3, 1), B(5, 1), C(5, 6) is rotated 90° anticlockwise to produce R'. What are the coordinates of R'?

Answers

1   a

$$\begin{pmatrix} 0 & -1 \\ -1 & 0 \end{pmatrix}\begin{pmatrix} 5 & 6 & 2 \\ 1 & 3 & 7 \end{pmatrix} = \begin{pmatrix} 0\times5+-1\times1 & 0\times6+-1\times3 & 0\times2+-1\times7 \\ -1\times5+0\times1 & -1\times6+0\times3 & -1\times2+0\times7 \end{pmatrix} = \begin{pmatrix} -1 & -3 & -7 \\ -5 & -6 & -2 \end{pmatrix}$$

Always put the transformation matrix first

Matrix for triangle T

Coordinates of T' are A'(–1, –5), B'(–3, –6), C'(–7, –2)

    b   Reflection in the line y = –x (see information on page 92)

2

$$\begin{pmatrix} 0 & -1 \\ 1 & 0 \end{pmatrix}$$ is the matrix to produce a rotation of 90° anticlockwise (see page 92)

$$\begin{pmatrix} 0 & -1 \\ 1 & 0 \end{pmatrix}\begin{pmatrix} 3 & 5 & 5 \\ 1 & 1 & 6 \end{pmatrix} = \begin{pmatrix} 0\times3+-1\times1 & 0\times5+-1\times1 & 0\times5+-1\times6 \\ 1\times3+0\times1 & 1\times5+0\times1 & 1\times5+0\times6 \end{pmatrix} = \begin{pmatrix} -1 & -1 & -6 \\ 3 & 5 & 5 \end{pmatrix}$$

Always put the transformation matrix first

Matrix for triangle R

Coordinates of R' are A'(–1, 3), B'(–1, 5), C'(–6, 5)

Important facts you are expected to know

Key words

Sum means **add**
Product means **multiply**

Units of measure

Length

10 millimetres (mm) = 1 centimetre (cm)
100 centimetres (cm) = 1 metre (m)
1000 metres (m) = 1 kilometre (km)

Mass

1000 grams (g) = 1 kilogram (kg)
1000 kilograms (kg) = 1 tonne (t)

Capacity

1000 cubic centimetres (cc) = 1 litre (l)
1000 millilitres (ml) = 1 litre (l)
100 centilitres (cl) = 1 litre (l)
10 millilitres (ml) = 1 centilitre (cl)

Significant figures

Rounding to one significant figure (1 sig. fig.)

3725 $\longrightarrow$ 4000 ⎫
28·63 $\longrightarrow$ 30 ⎬ Round to one figure, then add noughts to the decimal point. Do not add noughts after the decimal point.
421·3 $\longrightarrow$ 400 ⎭

Note: 421.3 does not become 400.0

0·038 $\longrightarrow$ 0·04 ⎫
0·724 $\longrightarrow$ 0·7 ⎬ Significant numbers are counted from the first non–zero figure.
0·0306 $\longrightarrow$ 0·03 ⎭

Continuous and discrete data

Discrete data is data which can only have certain values, eg the number of people in a room can only have whole number values. You cannot have 3.2 people in a room.

Continuous data is data which can have any value, eg distance between two places, height of a person. The height of a person can be measured to any degree of accuracy. A person could be 1.783642 m tall.

Formulae

You must memorise these formulae:

Circumference of a circle = $\quad 2\pi r = \pi d$
Area of a circle = $\quad \pi r^2$
Volume of a cylinder = $\quad \pi r^2 h$
Total surface area of a cylinder = $\quad 2\pi rh + 2\pi r^2$

Common error: Many errors are made by using the diameter instead of the radius.

Special triangles

You also need to know the special names of these two triangles:

Equilateral

An equilateral triangle has three axes of symmetry. If you fold on any axis of symmetry you produce two identical right-angled triangles.

Isosceles

Two sides equal. Two angles equal. An isosceles triangle has one axis of symmetry. If you fold on the axis of symmetry you produce two identical right-angled triangles.

Quadrilaterals

A quadrilateral is a four-sided shape. The angles add up to 360°. You are expected to know the following information about quadrilaterals.

Parallelogram

Opposite sides are parallel and the same length.
Opposite angles are equal.
Diagonals bisect each other.
Rotational symmetry order 2.

Rhombus

This is a parallelogram with four equal sides. Diagonals bisect each other. Rotational symmetry order 2.

Rectangle

A parallelogram with all angles equal (ie 90°).
Rotational symmetry order 2.

Square

A rectangle with all sides equal length.
Rotational symmetry order 4.

Trapezium

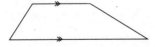

A quadrilateral with one pair of parallel sides.
No rotational symmetry.

Kite

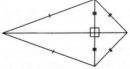

Two pairs of equal length sides adjacent to each other.
Diagonals cross at right-angles.
One diagonal bisects the other.
No rotational symmetry.

Regular polygons

A polygon is a shape made from straight lines. A regular polygon has all of its sides the same length and all of its angles the same size.

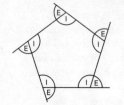

I = Interior angles
E = Exterior angles

The sum of the exterior angles of a polygon is 360°
Interior angle + exterior angle = 180°

Averages – mean and range

The **mean** is the most useful average because it uses all of the data.
The mean is sometimes called the arithmetic mean.
The **range** is the difference between the largest and smallest numbers.

Example
a   Find the mean of: 16, 18, 11, 19, 17   b   Find the range

Method
a   Add the numbers, then divide by how many numbers there are.

$$\frac{16 + 18 + 11 + 19 + 17}{5} = \frac{81}{5} = 16{\cdot}2$$

b   The range is 19 – 11 = 8

Averages – median and mode

The **median** is the middle number when the numbers are placed in order.
The **mode** is the most common number.

Examples
1   Find the median and mode of these numbers: 2, 3, 5, 3, 2, 4, 2
2   Find the median of these numbers: 7, 3, 10, 2
Method
1   First place the numbers in order of size

3 is the middle number, therefore the median is 3

2   2   2   3   3   4   5

There are more 2s than any other number, therefore the mode is 2

2   Place the numbers in order

2   3   7   10

The median is between 3 and 7

$$3 + \frac{7}{2} = \frac{10}{2} = 5$$

The median is 5

Number patterns

Examination questions often give you a pattern of numbers and ask you to describe the pattern.

Example

1 Describe how to find each term in the pattern 5, 8, 11, 14, 17
2 What is the tenth term?

Method

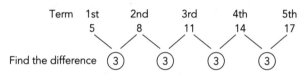

The difference is 3. This is what you multiply by:

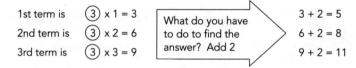

The rule is multiply the term by 3, then add 2. (In algebraic terms this is $3n + 2$.)
The tenth term is $3 \times 10 + 2 = 32$

Diagnostic tests

These tests will help you check how good you are at questions on each topic. If you have difficulty, revise the topic again.

1 **Rational and irrational numbers**
State whether each number is rational or irrational. If the number is rational write the number in the form $^a/_b$.
  1 $0.21\dot{7}$ 2 $\sqrt{7}$
  3 $\sqrt{25}$ 4 5π
  5 0.481

2 **Using a calculator: Brackets, memory and fractions**
  1 $6.41(3.72 - 8.532)$
  2 $\dfrac{6.87 - (9.36 \times 3.4)}{8.42 \times 0.164}$

3 **Using a calculator: Powers, roots and memory**
  1 A cube has a volume of 216 cm³. What is the length of each side?
  2 What is the value of 5^4?
  3 Calculate the value of:
     a $2401^{3/4}$ b $^5\sqrt{243}$

4 **Standard form**
  1 Write 6.32×10^{-4} as an ordinary number.
  2 Write 273 000 in standard form.
  3 Write 0.0072 in standard form.
  4 $8.42 \times 10^{-6} \div 3.4 \times 10^{-2}$

5 **Percentages and fractions**
  1 A cinema holds 3200 people. Safety regulations require the capacity to be reduced by $^3/_8$. What is the capacity after the reduction?
  2 Mrs Saunders earned £240 per week. She received a 6% increase. What was her wage after the increase?

3 Mr Williams earned £180 per week in 1990. He received a 4% rise each year for five years. Calculate his wage in 1995.

4 Miss Soames bought a car for £10 000. The car depreciated by 10% each year. How much was it worth after four years?

6 **Calculating growth and decay rates**
The value of an antique vase increases by 4% each year. Its value in 1990 was £2704.
  a Calculate its value in 1996 to the nearest pound.
  b Calculate its value in 1988.

7 **Patterns you must recognise**
  1 What are the special names given to these numbers?
     a 1, 4, 9, 16, 25, 36...
     b 1, 8, 27, 64, 125, 216...
     c 1, 3, 6, 10, 15, 21...
  2 List the factors of 30.
  3 Complete the next three prime numbers:
     2, 3, 5, 7...

8 **Product of primes, highest common factor, lowest common multiple and reciprocals**
  1 Write 1960 as a product of primes.
  2 Find the HCF and LCM of 36 and 90.
  3 Find the reciprocal of –8.

9 Trial and improvement

Find the value of x correct to one decimal place using trial and improvement. You must show all of your working.

$$x^3 + x = 108$$

10 Equations

Solve these equations. Give the answer correct to three significant figures where appropriate.

1 $y^2 = 10$

2 $\sqrt{y} = 17$

3 $^5/y = 8$

4 $3(y + 6) - 2(4y - 1) = 8$

11 Rewriting formulae

Make y the subject:

1 $\sqrt{y} = 4c$

2 $y^2 = 25x^2$

3 $^A/_y = B$

12 Iteration

1 Produce two iterative formulae for $x^2 + 7x + 13 = 0$

2 The iterative formula

$$x_{n+1} = \frac{15}{x_n} + 2$$

can be used to solve the equation $x^2 - 2x - 15 = 0$. Use the iterative formula to find a solution to the equation. Start with $x_1 = 7$.

13 Direct and inverse variation

a is proportional to c^3

a = 50 when c = 2

1 Find a when c = 10

2 Find c when a = 400

14 Using algebraic formulae

$a = \frac{1}{5}$, b = 2·3, c = -3·7, d = $-\frac{4}{5}$

Find the value of:

1 6(4a - 3d)

2 $\sqrt{\left(\dfrac{a^2 + b^2}{-3c}\right)}$

3 $\left(\dfrac{3a^2 + b^2}{c^2 - d}\right)$

4 $v = \pi r^2 h$

  a Calculate v when r = 3, h = 4

  b Calculate h when r = 10, v = 400

  c Calculate r when h = 5, v = 300

15 Rules for indices (powers)

Simplify:

1 $y^{1/4} \times y^{1/3}$

2 $y^{1/3} \div y^{-1/2}$

3 Evaluate $\dfrac{1}{4}^{-2}$

16 Expansion of brackets

Simplify:

1 $a^5 \times a^3$

2 $4a^4 \times 3a$

3 $8a^6 \div 2a^{-4}$

Expand:

4 $5a(4a^2x - 3ac)$

5 $2a^2c^3(3ad^2 + 4a^2c)$

6 $(2a - 4)(3a - 5)$

17-19 Factorisation

Factorise:

1 $12a^2 - 4ac$

2 $15a^2c^2d + 25a^3c$

3 $a^2 - 7a + 10$

4 Solve $a^2 - 7a + 10 = 0$

20 Solving quadratic equations

1 Solve $y^2 = 3y + 5$. Give your answer correct to 3 significant figures.

21 Simultaneous equations: Solving using algebra

Solve the simultaneous equations

$3a - 2y = 16$ and $5a - 3y = 26$

22-23 Simplifying algebraic fractions

1 Simplify $\dfrac{15x + 20}{6x + 8}$

2 Simplify $\dfrac{8a^3c^2}{3ad^2} \div \dfrac{4ac^5}{9a^2c}$

24 Drawing lines

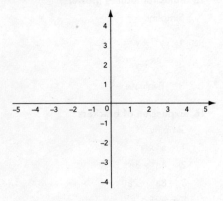

Draw and label the following lines

1 $y = 0$ 2 $x = 0$
3 $y = 4$ 4 $x = -3$
5 $y = x$ 6 $y = -x$

25 Simultaneous equations: Solving by drawing a graph

1 Solve the pair of simultaneous equations by drawing a graph.

$2y - x = 6$ $y + 2x = 8$

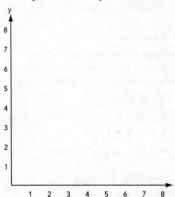

26 Solving equations using graphical methods

Use graphical methods to solve $x^2 - 5x + 6 = 0$. Plot your graph for $-1 \leq x \leq 4$

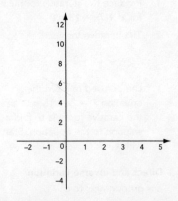

27 The straight line equation $y = mx + c$

What is the equation of the line which passes through the points $(2,0)$ and $(6,6)$?

28 Using tangents to find gradients

Draw a graph of $y = x^2$ for $-3 \leq x \leq 3$.

Find the gradient at:

a $x = -2$ b $x = 1$

c $x = 2$

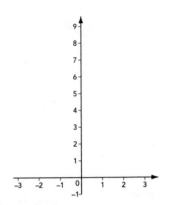

29-30 Expressing general rules in symbolic form

This table shows the labour costs of having a cooker repaired. It consists of a fixed rate call-out charge plus a charge per half hour.

Time (min)	30	60	90	120
Cost (£)	20	28		44

1 Draw a graph to show this information (time on the horizontal axis, cost on the vertical axis).

2 What is the fixed rate call-out charge?

3 Find a formula connecting the labour cost (C) in pounds and the time (T) in hours.

4 Use your graph to estimate the cost for 90 minutes and hence complete the table.

5 Use your formula to find the cost for 180 minutes.

31 Drawing graphs

Label the following graphs.

Choose from:

$y = 2x^2 + 2$

$y = -3x^2 + 2$

$y = 2x + 2$

$y = -2x + 2$

$y = {}^1\!/x$

$y = {}^{-1}\!/x$

$y = x^3$

$y = -x^3$

a

b

c

32-33 Sketching graphs

This is the graph of $y = f(x)$.
Sketch the graphs of:

a $y = f(x + 2)$

b $y = f(x) + 2$

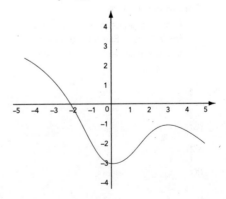

34 Speed, time and distance graphs

This graph shows the journey made by a car from Poole to Basingstoke:

1   What time did the car arrive in Basingstoke?

2   What was the speed of the car on the first part of its journey?

3   The car stayed in Basingstoke for half an hour and then returned to Poole at the speed of 40 km/h.

a   Complete the graph

b   What time did the car arrive back in Poole?

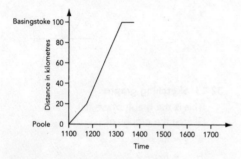

35 Area under a curve

1   Draw the graph of $y = \frac{1}{2}x^2 + 2x$ for $0 \le x \le 6$. Estimate the area under the curve by using three trapezia.

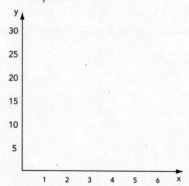

36 Intersecting and parallel lines

Look at the diagram below.

1   Find the size of the missing angles.

2   What are the special mathematical names for:

a   angles c and d?

b   angles a and d?

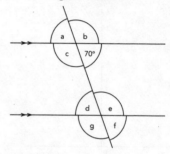

37 Bearings

In the diagram below, A, B and C are three ships.

1   What is the bearing of A from B?

2   What is the bearing of B from A?

3   What is the bearing of B from C?

A ·

N
↑

· B

˙C

38 Similarity

AC = 10 cm   BC = 12 cm

AD = 6 cm   DE = 9 cm

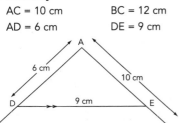

Find the length of:

1   AE

2   AB

3   BD

39-40 Congruent triangles

Look at these pairs of triangles. Are they congruent? If so give a reason.

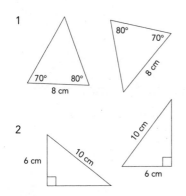

41 Combined and inverse transformations

1   A shape X is translated by the vector $\begin{pmatrix} 3 \\ 7 \end{pmatrix}$ to produce X'. Describe the transformation to return X' to X.

2   A shape H is reflected in the line x = 3 to produce H'. Describe the transformation to return H' to H.

42-43 Enlargement by a fractional scale factor and a negative scale factor

1   Enlarge the triangle A by a scale factor of $\frac{1}{2}$. Centre of enlargement is the point (7,3).

2   Enlarge the triangle A by a scale factor of –2, centre of enlargement is the point (1, 0).

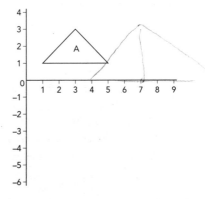

44 Compound measures

1   A car travels 324 kilometres in 3 hours 52 minutes. Calculate the speed in kilometres per hour.

2   A car travels at 25 metres per second. What is this speed in kilometres per hour?

45 Time

1. A ferry leaves Poole at 21:47 on Wednesday and arrives in Cherbourg at 06:18 on Thursday. How long did the journey take?

2. A car travels 321 kilometres at an average speed of 57 km/h. How long does the journey take? Give your answer to:

   a the nearest minute

   b the nearest second.

46-47 Upper and lower bounds of numbers

1. 3·24 is correct to two decimal places. What is:

   a the maximum possible value?

   b the minimum possible value?

2. All numbers are correct to one decimal place, find:

   a the maximum possible value

   b the minimum possible value of

   $$\frac{3 \cdot 6 + 1 \cdot 7}{2 \cdot 9 - 1 \cdot 3}$$

48 Length, area and volume of shapes with curves

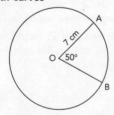

1. Find the length of the minor arc AB

2. Find the length of the major arc AB

3. Find the area of the sector OAB

49-51 Angle and tangent properties of circles

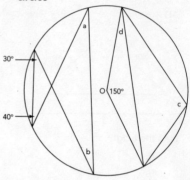

Find a, b, c, d

52 Calculating length, area and volume – 1

1. Calculate the area:

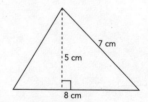

2. Calculate the area:

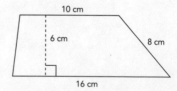

3. The volume of a cuboid is 144 cm^3. The length is 8 cm, the width is 6 cm. Calculate the height.

53 Calculating length, area and volume – 2

Find the volume of these shapes.

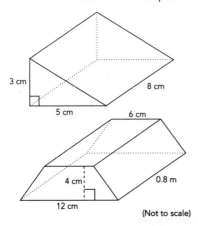

3 cm

8 cm

5 cm

6 cm

4 cm

0.8 m

12 cm

(Not to scale)

54 Calculating length, area and volume – 3

Find:

1 the area and

2 the perimeter of this shape.

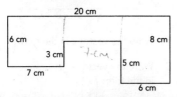

20 cm

6 cm

8 cm

3 cm

5 cm

7 cm

6 cm

55 Formulae for length, area and volume

a, b, c and d are lengths. State whether each formula gives a length, area, volume or none of these:

1 $4\pi r$ 2 $3ab$

3 $abc + d$

4 $\dfrac{abc}{d^2}$ 5 $\dfrac{a^2bc}{d}$

56 Ratio for length, area and volume

1 The ratio of the volume of cube A to cube B is 512 : 343.

What is the ratio of the side of cube A to cube B?

2 Convert 0.3 m^2 into cm^2

57 Pythagoras' theorem

1 Find x

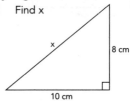

x

8 cm

10 cm

2 Find y

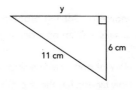

y

6 cm

11 cm

58 Trigonometry: Finding an angle

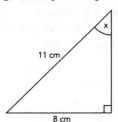

x

11 cm

8 cm

59 Trigonometry: Finding a side

1 Find x

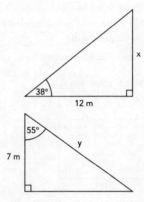

2 Find y

60 Trigonometry: Solving problems

A ship sails 300 km on a bearing of 078°.

1 How far north has the ship sailed?

2 How far east has the ship sailed?

61 Trigonometry and Pythagoras' theorem for 3-D shapes

1 Find the distance from B to H

2 Find the angle BHF

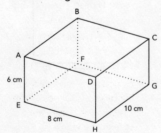

62-64 Sine, cosine and tangent of any angle

Cosx = –0·7313537. Find the values of x between 0° and 360°

65-66 Sine rule, cosine rule, area of a triangle

1 Find x

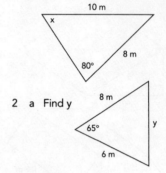

2 a Find y

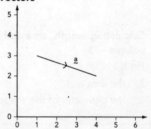

b Find the area

67-70 Vectors

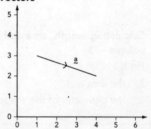

1 Write the vector $\underset{\sim}{a}$ in the form $\begin{pmatrix} x \\ y \end{pmatrix}$

2 Write the vector $-3\underset{\sim}{a}$ in the form $\begin{pmatrix} x \\ y \end{pmatrix}$

3 Vector $\underset{\sim}{a}$ + vector $\underset{\sim}{b}$ = $\begin{pmatrix} 5 \\ 4 \end{pmatrix}$. Find vector $\underset{\sim}{b}$.

71 Locus

1 Two points, A and B are 5 cm apart. Draw the locus of the point which is always an equal distance from A and B.

A ·   · B

2 This is a plan of a building. The building has a force-field which reaches 20 m from the building. The scale is 1 cm represent 20 m. Use a dotted line to show the edge of the force field. Part of the force field is drawn for you

----
Force field

Building

72 Designing questionnaires

1 State one advantage and one disadvantage of asking this question:

Which is your favourite subject?

2 State one advantage and one disadvantage of asking this question:

Place a tick by your favourite subject from this list	
Maths	
English	
French	
History	
Science	

73 Sampling

Criticise this sampling technique:

A school had 30 teachers, 400 boys and 300 girls. A survey was conducted to find the most popular school meal. Five teachers, five boys and five girls were interviewed.

74 Hypotheses

1 Kim tests the hypothesis "Boys watch more television than girls" by conducting a survey.

She could present the results in a bar chart. Write down four other ways in which she could present the data.

2 How would you test these hypotheses? Choose from experiment, observation or questionnaire:

a Boys' favourite colour is blue.

b A certain die is biased.

c Red is the most common colour for cars.

75 Comparing data

Draw a frequency polygon to illustrate the following data. Compare the distributions and comment on your findings. This table shows the rainfall in two towns. (Rainfall is in millimetres.)

Month	Hilton	Deepdale
April	20	12
May	18	15
June	16	25
July	15	32
August	15	26
September	16	18

76 Histograms

This histogram shows the ages of people in a theatre:

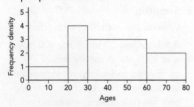

1   How many people are aged 0-20?
2   How many people are aged 20-30?
3   How many people are aged over 30?

77 Grouped data

This table shows the marks obtained by 200 students in an examination:

Mark	0-20	21-40	41-60	61-80	81-100
Frequency	0	68	36	54	42

1   What is the modal class?
2   Estimate the median.
3   Estimate the mean.

78 Cumulative frequency

This table shows the heights of 80 boys aged 15 at Upton School:

Height (cm)	Frequency
150 to 160	5
160 to 170	8
170 to 180	26
180 to 190	37
190 to 200	4

1   What is the range of the heights?
2   Draw a cumulative frequency diagram.
3   What is the median height?
4   What is the upper quartile?
5   What is the lower quartile?
6   What is the interquartile range?

79 Using cumulative frequency diagrams to compare distributions

This table shows the heights of 100 boys aged 15 at Downland School:

Height (cm)	Frequency
150 to 160	17
160 to 170	21
170 to 180	23
180 to 190	18
190 to 200	21

Draw a cumulative frequency diagram to show this information. Use the median and interquartile range to compare the boys at Downland School with the boys at Upton School in the previous question.

80 Standard deviation

Find the standard deviation of these numbers: 7, 8, 14, 15, 20

81 The normal distribution

A factory produces planks of wood. The planks are normally distributed with a mean length of 85 cm and a standard deviation of 0·05 cm.

1   What are the lengths between which the central 68% should lie?

2   If a plank of wood is more than two standard deciations below the mean it is rejected. What is the rejection length?

82 Line of best fit

This scatter diagram shows the height and mass of eight girls aged 15:

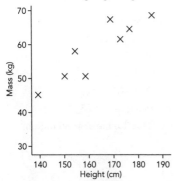

1   Describe the relationship shown by this graph.

2   Draw a line of best fit.

3   Use your line of best fit to estimate the mass of another 15 year old girl who is 170 cm tall.

83 Estimation of probability by experiment

Sarah and Jane tried an experiment. They each dropped drawing-pins from a height of 2 m. This table shows how they landed:

	Point up	Point down
Sarah	6	4
Jane	40	60

1   Which results are likely to be most reliable and why?

2   Using Jane's results estimate the number of "point up" you would expect if the experiment was carried out 10 000 times.

84 Tree diagrams

John has a 0·3 chance of passing History and a 0·4 chance of passing Geography. Draw a tree diagram to show this and hence calculate:

1   His probability of passing both subjects.

2   His probability of passing exactly one subject.

3   His probability of failing both subjects.

85 Conditional and independent probability

The probability of Monday being dry is 0·6. If Monday is dry the probability of Tuesday being dry is 0·8. If Monday is wet the probability of Tuesday being dry is 0·4.

1 Show this in a tree diagram

2 What is the probability of both days being dry?

3 What is the probability of both days being wet?

4 What is the probability of exactly one dry day?

86-87 Probability

1 A bag contains four red discs, four blue discs and two yellow discs. A girl is blindfolded and selects a disc. Discs are not replaced. What is the probability of selecting:

a A red disc?

b A yellow disc?

c A red or a yellow disc?

d Two red discs?

e One red disc and one yellow disc in any order?

2 Four coins are tossed. What is the probability of at least one head?

Supplementary material

88 3-D co-ordinates

A cuboid has the following co-ordinates:

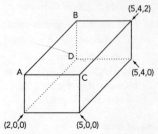

What are the co-ordinates of A, B, C and D?

89 Inequalities

Solve these inequalities:

1 $6x < 24$

2 $x - 3 > -5$

3 $-3x \leq -12$

4 $14 \leq 3x - 1 < 23$

5 Describe the shaded region.

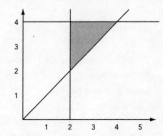

Answers to diagnostic tests

1

1 Rational $^{217}/_{999}$ 2 Irrational

3 Rational 5 or $^5/_1$ 4 Irrational

5 Rational $^{481}/_{1000}$

2

1 -30·84492   2 -18·071085

3

1 6 cm   2 625

3 a 343   b 3

4

1 0·000632   2 2·73 x 10^5

3 7·2 x 10^{-3} 4 2·476 x 10^{-4}

                     or 0·0002476

5

1 2000   2 £254·40

            (Note: £254·4 is wrong)

3 £219   4 £6561

6

1 a £3421   b £2500

7

1 a Square numbers

   b Cube numbers

   c Triangle numbers

2 1, 2, 3, 5, 6, 10, 15, 30

3 11, 13, 17

8

1 2 x 2 x 2 x 5 x 7 x 7 or $2^3.5.7^2$

2 HCF 18

   LCM 180

3 $-^1/_8$ or $-0·125$

9

1 4·7

10

1 3·16   2 289

3 0·625   4 2·4

11

1 $y = (4c)^2$ or $y = 16c^2$

2 $y = 5x$

3 $y = {}^A/_8$

12

1 $x_{n+1} = \dfrac{-13}{x_n + 7}$ and $x_{n+1} = \dfrac{-13}{x_n} - 7$

2 $x = 5$

13

1 6250

2 4 [note: k = 6·25]

14

1 19·2   2 0·69295

3 0·37336   4 a 113

                          b 1·27

                          c 4·37

15

1 $y^{1/_{12}}$ 2 $y^{5/_6}$

3 16

16

1 a^8 2 $12a^5$

3 $4a^{10}$ 4 $20a^3x - 15a^2c$

5 $6a^3c^3d^2 + 8a^4c^4$ 6 $6a^2 - 22a + 20$

17-19

1 $4a(3a - c)$ 2 $5a^2c(3cd + 5a)$

3 $(a - 5)(a - 2)$ 4 $a = 5, 2$

20

Using the formula gives $y = 4·19$ or $y = -1·19$

21

$a = 4, y = -2$

22-23

1 $\dfrac{5(3x + 4)}{2(3x + 4)} = \dfrac{5}{2}$ 2 $\dfrac{6a^3}{c^2d^2}$

Answers

24

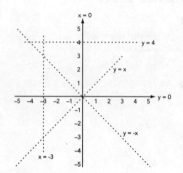

25

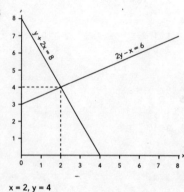

x = 2, y = 4

26

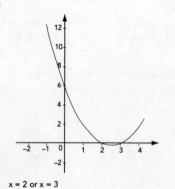

x = 2 or x = 3

27

$y = {}^{3}/_{2}x - 3$

28

(You should have similar, but not exact answers)

1   a   -4   b   2

    c   4

29-30

1   Assume your graph is correct if your answers are correct

2   £12   3   C = 12 +16T

4   £36   5   £60

31

a $y = 2x + 2$ b $y = -3x^2 + 2$

c $y = -x^3$

32-33

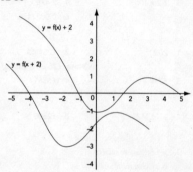

34

1   13·15

2   27 km/h (approx) (see diagram)

3   a

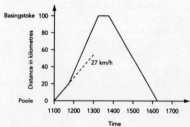

    b   16:15

35

    71

Answers

36

1 a = 70°   2a Alternate
   b = 110°   b Corresponding
   c = 110°
   d = 70°
   e = 110°
   f = 70°
   g = 110°

37

1 286°   2 106°
3 056°

38

1 7·5 cm   2 8 cm
3 2 cm

39-40

1 Not congruent
2 Congruent RHS

41

1 Translation by the vector $\begin{pmatrix} -3 \\ -7 \end{pmatrix}$
2 Reflection in the line x = 3

42-43

1 (4, 2), (5, 3), (6, 2)
2 (1, −2), (5, −6), (9, −2)

44

1 83·79 km/h   2 90 km/h

45

1 8 hours 31 minutes
2 a 5 hours 38 minutes
   b 5 hours 37 minutes 54 seconds

46-47

1 a 3·245   b 3·235
2 a 3·6   b 3·0588

48

1 6·11 cm   2 37·9 cm
3 21·4 cm^2

49-51

a 30°   b 40°
c 105°   d 15°

52

1 20 cm^2 2 78 cm^2
3 3 cm

53

1 60 cm^3
2 2880 cm^3 or 0·00288 m^3

54

1 111 cm^2
2 62 cm

55

1 Length   2 Area
3 None of these   4 Length
5 Volume

56

1 8 : 7   2 3000 cm^2

57

1 12·8 cm   2 9·22 cm

58

46·7°

59

1 9·38 m   2 12·2 m

60

1 62·4 km   2 293 km

61

1 14·1 cm   2 25·1°

62-64

137° and 223°

65-66

1 52·0°
2 a 7·71 m   b 21·8 m^2

67-70

1 $\begin{pmatrix} 3 \\ -1 \end{pmatrix}$ 2 $\begin{pmatrix} -9 \\ 3 \end{pmatrix}$

3 $\begin{pmatrix} 2 \\ 5 \end{pmatrix}$

Answers

71

1

2

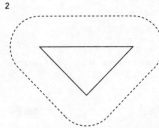

72

1 It is an open-ended question. Pupils can state their favourite subject (advantage). There may be a large number of different responses. These may be difficult to analyse and record (disadvantage).

2 It is a closed question. The subject chosen is only the favourite from the list, so it may not be the pupil's favourite (disadvantage). There are only five possible responses. This will make it easy to analyse and record the results (advantage).

73

1 The sample is not large enough.

2 This is not a representative sample (eg there are more boys than teachers, the sample must reflect this). A representative sample could be 3 teachers, 40 boys, 30 girls.

74

1 Table, pie chart, frequency polygon, pictogram

2 a Questionnaire
  b Experiment
  c Observation

75

Hilton has a similar amount of rainfall each month, the rainfall varies in Deepdale with more rain in the middle months of June, July and August. Deepdale has more rainfall than Hilton.

76

1 20   2 40
3 130

77

1 21-40   2 58 (approx)
3 57 (approx)

78

1 50

2

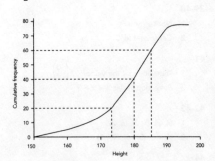

3 181 (approx)   4 186 (approx)
5 173 (approx)   6 13 (approx)

79

Downland

Median = 175 (approx), upper quartile = 188 (approx), lower quartile = 164 (approx), interquartile range = 24 (approx)

The median shows the middle boy at Upton School is 6 cm taller.

The interquartile range at Downland School is 24, at Upland 13. This shows the boys at Upland School vary less in height than the boys at Downland School (ie they are more closely grouped at Upland School).

80

4·79

81

1 84·95 cm and 85·05 cm

2 Below 84·9 cm

82

1 Positive corellation, or the taller the heavier

2 Line from about (140, 45) to (190, 70)

3 60 kg (approx)

83

1 Jane's results, because she carried out the experiment more times

2 4000

84

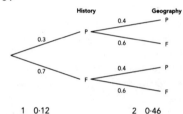

1 0·12   2 0·46

3 0·42

85

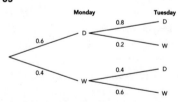

2 0·6 x 0·8 = 0·48

3 0·4 x 0·6 = 0·24

4 0·6 x 0·2 + 0·4 x 0·4 = 0·28

86-87

1 a $^4/_{10} = ^2/_5$

   b $^2/_{10} = ^1/_5$

   c $^6/_{10} = ^3/_5$

   d $^2/_{15}$

   e $^8/_{45}$

2 $^{15}/_{16}$

88

A = (2,0,2), B = (2,4,2), C = (5,0,2), D = (2,4,0)

89

1 x < 4   2 x > -2

3 x ≥ 4   4 5 ≤ x < 8

5 x ≥ 2, y < 4, y > x

Index